The Ethics Of Euripides

THE ETHICS OF EURIPIDES

COLUMBIA UNIVERSITY PRESS

SALES AGENTS

NEW YORK:
LEMCKE & BUECHNER
30-32 WEST 27TH STREET

LONDON:
HUMPHREY MILFORD
AMEN CORNER, E.C.

THE
ETHICS OF EURIPIDES

BY

RHYS CARPENTER

M.A. (OXON.), PH.D.

ARCHIVES OF PHILOSOPHY

EDITED BY

FREDERICK J. E. WOODBRIDGE

No. 7, MAY, 1916

New York

COLUMBIA UNIVERSITY PRESS

1916

88 EF
C22

THE ETHICS OF EURIPIDES

CHAPTER I

τὸ δὲ φυᾷ κράτιστον ἅπαν. "Nature's way is ever the strongest and best," wrote Pindar in his ninth Olympian ode.[1] Like much of his teaching, the aphorism has more earnestness than originality. Indeed, it is as a commonplace of Greek conviction that I have chosen it as my starting-point and text. If it were possible to comprise in one short sentence the essential differences of the Greek genius from that of other nations and of modern times, Pindar might claim to have come near to that achievement. For there is an entire world — an entire Greek world — of meaning in φυᾷ. It implies that the Greek standard, the ethical and physical sanction, is not drawn from a supra-mundane or transcendental source, but from the physical world as it is or as it tends to be.

τὸ δὲ φυᾷ κράτιστον ἅπαν. Hence, in logic, the Platonic theory of ideas, inasmuch as the idea can be defined as that form of any *infima species* which is wholly and perfectly φυᾷ. The logical concept to the Greeks had always a curious concreteness. It was not an abstraction so much as a formal visualisation of the object in its complete and perfect state. Hence that curious dualism in Plato, — a world of objects, and a world of ideas which always threatened to be objects also. τὸ δὲ φυᾷ κράτιστον ἅπαν: the ideas were the objects φυᾷ, and as such they had a particular κράτος or δύναμις, a driving power directing these material counterparts toward the perfection which should be theirs by nature.

In sculpture, that strange early development through a very limited number of fixed types is common to most early art, inasmuch as differentiation is a late acquirement. But note that the types did not stagnate into conventions, as seems to have happened occasionally in Egypt and many Oriental countries. The sculptor was never satisfied with his heritage, because he felt very vividly, "τὸ φυᾷ κράτιστον ἅπαν." Fifth-century athletic art is an amazing blend of geometric formalism and realistic observation: the former (inherited from the archaic schema)

---

[1] Ol. ix. 107.

gives it the so-called classic regularity and "suppression" of unessentials; the realism saves it from conventionalisation. Greek art is a spiritual interpretation of the physical. But what that phrase means, only those will understand who realise that the generations of sculptors were studying the nude athlete in order to find that schema toward which Nature is striving without ever a perfect attainment. They worked toward the human form φυᾷ, the bodily εἶδος, and not toward a mere counterpart of this Olympic athlete here and now. It is the bare truth to call Greek sculpture Platonic, in spite of all Plato's strictures on art. The canonic statue of an athlete is the visible presentation of the Platonic Idea of the athlete. Both are imaginary, yet deduced from reality, from the multitudinous members of the species, each of which is more or less completely φυᾷ. Greek sculpture was thus for long confined by the demands of a strict development toward a logical concept. For that reason, in comparison with modern art, it impresses the unspecialized as strangely limited in imaginativeness, or, better, in that particular quality of imaginative suggestiveness which may be termed phantasy, whose stimulus is through strong emotional vagueness. Maxfield Parrish's scenes from Greek mythology, for instance, or Gilbert Murray's reimbodiments of Euripidean tragedy, are full of this modern appeal, of which Hellenic art knows so little. Compare these two versions (both of them in my judgment good poetry):

> . . . ἐμὲ δὲ πόντιον σκάφος
> ἀίσσον πτεροῖσι πορεύσει
> ἱππόβοτον Ἄργος, ἵνα τείχεα
> λάϊνα Κυκλώπι' οὐράνια νέμονται.
>
> (Tro. 1085–8)

> " . . . and me the ships
> Shall bear o'er the bitter brine,
>   Storm-birds upon angry pinions,
> Where the towers of the Giants shine
>   O'er Argos cloudily,
> And the riders ride by the sea."

In the Greek, every picture is single and concise, and refers to places and conditions actually known to the hearers. In the English, the whole effect counts upon vague pictures, indefinite plurals, unfamiliar places, and unknown men.

It has been suggested to me that I am wrong in entirely denying to the Greek this sense of imaginative appeal and that, for example, we

derive a very modern emotional stimulus from the vase-painting of
the morning-stars who dive through the clouds at the approach of
the sun.[2]

I might, of course, plead that an instance so unique is eloquent of
the prevalence of the opposite condition. But I am inclined rather to
question the validity of the example; for, were the mythology as much
a commonplace to us as to the Greeks, the illustration of the stars as
youths would have no more imaginative stimulus than a statue of Apollo
as a young man. I mean that there are no vague suggestions, no half-
lights nor lowering shadows, such as the Romanticists and the Celt-
icists have made familiar. For, all these effects are obtained by a play
on Nature, a suppression, a distortion, an exaggeration, an innuendo
of the unusual and mysterious, a trick of the half-seen, the imperfect.
But if to the Greek τὸ φυᾷ κράτιστον ἅπαν, then art is at its best when it
is at its most precise. And thus, in its most serious and noble work,
instead of imaginative surprises with their unbalanced emphasis, there
is the strictest subordination of every element in its just and logical
position. I do not believe that the specialist in Greek art will dispute
the real tyranny of this almost logical formulation; yet, for additional
support, a reference may be permitted to the Pythagorean-like formalism
in such strangely arithmetical creatures as the "canons." Greek archi-
tecture and apparently certain periods of Greek sculpture placed an
almost fanatical trust in the efficacy of pure numerical ratio, and when
Diogenes Laertius says of the sculptor Pythagoras of Rhegium that he
was the first to use συμμετρία, I hold it obvious that the word cannot
be translated "symmetry," but refers to the observance of arithmetical ratios between the various physical members. Derived, as this
procedure seems to have been, from mathematico-physical and musical
speculations on Nature's supposed inherent preference for simple numerical ratios,[3] it reveals the Greek artist in an effort to catch Nature's
own ideal and to show in stone that which is perfectly φυᾷ.

Again, in Greek ethical thought, Pindar's gnome finds a wide application. Since conclusions here are especially open to challenge as hasty
or superficial impressions, I make a more exhaustive appeal to particu-
lars, in order to show that Pindar's gnome is the key-note to Euripides'
morality and that the logical concept is quite as dominant there as in
Greek sculpture. To be sure, one can scarcely demand a rigorous proof

---

[2] Furtwängler-Reichhold-Hauser, *Griechische Vasenmalerei*, III, pl. 126.

[3] Cf. Arist. de Caelo. F. 1. 300a 16. ἔνιοι γὰρ τὴν φύσιν ἐξ ἀριθμῶν συνιστᾶσιν,
ὥσπερ τῶν Πυθαγορείων τινές. Cf. also Arist. Met. A. ch. 5.

extracted from a dramatist, who by profession holds up his mirror to a changeful and inconsistent world. And yet, as I hope to show, his ethic has in reality just this rigor, if one but apprehend the ἀνυπόθετος ἀρχή, the self-sufficient and self-evident principle from which all his specific rules of conduct are deducible.

If one reads Euripides with this in view, the plays seem to conspire to emphasise a certain single ethical principle. This they exemplify in its different applications to the stuff of tragedy and human life. In fact this principle is so insistent, so explanatory of the meaning of the plays, that it runs like a *forma informans* through Euripides' dramas, as effective in his moral thought as symmetry was in the work of the sculptor of pediments or isocephalism for the early designer of relief.

The principle of which I am speaking is a tacit assumption at the back of Greek ethic generally and is its source of moral sanction. Precisely because it is basic it is seldom found expressed in Greek writers. But though the fundamental postulates of a nation's way of thought are not expressed, because they are never seen against a contrasting background, yet every honest utterance betrays them.

For the ethical principle in question, one may assume some variant of Pindar's gnome, such as, τὸ ζῆν κατὰ φύσιν ἐστὶν εὖ ζῆν.[4] An English equivalent for the phrase can scarcely be said to exist. For that reason, and because clarity in terms is vital for my thesis, a more detailed analysis of the wording is essential.

φύσις is the world in which we are; not, however, the world as a haphazard congeries of matter, but as a great ordered system of organic things in growth, attained development, and decay. The world must be realised to be under law, before φύσις can be understood. The various kinds of plants differ from one another: they have different φύσις. The laws of growth keep them relentlessly to their own development, their own nature. A rose differs from a violet because of φύσις. But one rose differs also from another rose. No two members of an *ultima species* are precisely alike. What is it that makes them different? Scarcely their φύσις, for the φύσις of a rose is always the same. There are other forces at work, and these operate against the φύσις, they are παρὰ φύσιν. If everything in this world were strictly κατὰ φύσιν, every rose would be like every other one and all alike would be *perfect* roses. Unhampered φύσις would develop every nascent organism into a perfect exemplification of its type, its εἶδος. The type or εἶδος is a static conception; φύσις

----

[4] Cf. Diog. Laert. viii. 87. διόπερ τέλος γίνεται τὸ ἀκολούθως τῇ φύσει ζῆν.

is dynamic, it is the complex of laws by which everything tends to attain its εἶδος.[5]

A good rose must have, let us say, its full quota of petals. The literal moth and the figurative rust must not have worked it harm. It must have had sun and rain. φύσις must have had full play, that from the seed it might develop stalk and leaf and bud and perfect flower. Only so can it attain its full type, its εἶδος. A good rose is a perfect rose. It is wholly κατὰ φύσιν.

Man is in a like position. Only, with him, development is not mere physical growth. The whole complex of mental and spiritual powers must expand and increase to their perfect form. Yet we can say of him what we said of the rose. As a good rose is a perfect rose, so a good man is a perfect man. He must be wholly κατὰ φύσιν. He must, under the unobstructed action of φύσις, attain his εἶδος as material organism, as sentient animal, and as thinking man. In so far as he exerts his powers to further this action of φύσις, he is acting rightly; in so far as he thwarts φύσις, he is acting wrongly.

Back of such an attitude of the Greek mind there must have been an extraordinary sense for the community between man and the rest of the material world. The modern mind opposes itself to Nature. With our artificialities of living and thinking, our exotic scientific diversion of natural forces, we feel that we dominate her. The supremacy of Mind marks us out from our surroundings: we feel like powerful strangers from another planet who have seized upon this earth, thanks to our unterrestrial sagacity. The Greek could not have felt so. He was part of the natural world, as plants and animals were part of it, though with a more intimate insight because of his part in its intellectual aspect.[6] To such a people it is not a great imaginative and poetic flight to feel that man is like the flowers of the field. It is merely a simple statement of an obvious truth.

Secondly, the Greek must have had a keen eye for formal perfection and have realized that every organism under favourable conditions develops a product which has a formal, as well as a purely material,

[5] But it is also the *matter* upon which that εἶδος is formed. Burnet in his recent book, *Greek Philosophy from Thales to Plato*, justly emphasises this aspect of the meaning of the word in the vocabulary of a slightly earlier period. (Cf. *o. c.* p. 27.)

[6] I do not mean that he was the care-free child of nature, the pastoral fiction of an 18th century imagination. Minds like that of Aeschylus, who was thoroughly Greek, are a sufficient contradiction to such generalities. But there is an ultimate *Versöhnung*, not an ultimate opposition, between man and the high mysteries of Nature. ἄτη acts παρὰ φύσιν and its catastrophe is so best explained.

significance. Nature, we might say, has a love of pure form. (Not that she displays a conscious aesthetic interest: there may be very simple reasons why Nature tends toward a formal articulation. For one thing, it is probably mechanically easier: at least, symmetry is mathematically simpler than asymmetry.) Rather, I wish to emphasise the mere empirical fact that Nature constantly strives toward a *formal* expression. The botanist, the zoologist, the biologist knows this. The Greek seems to have been peculiarly sensitive to it.

There results a certain optimistic confidence in Nature. Unthwarted φύσις produces, as far as form goes, superior and more perfect products. Thwart Nature, and consider the undergrown or crippled or uneven results. Formally, they are far inferior. But give the rose its proper soil and dew and sunlight, and the perfect form appears; and give to men the soil of individual freedom, the dew of material self-sufficiency, and the sunlight of good fortune, and they likewise will attain their formal and natural perfection.

A gardener working in a sandy and barren soil would not be prone to emphasise this striving toward form. His flowers would all be imperfect, with stunted stem, uneven leaf, and ill-developed blossom. So amid the misery of the ghetto, the rabble of the dusty streets of Alexandria, or the ill-fed slave-hordes of imperial Rome, in certain more unfavorable periods, the Greek doctrine would have little meaning and make little appeal. But the Greeks of the Euripidean age were an individualistic aristocracy. From their slave-tilled soil they sprang up independent and self-sufficient. Inside their city-fatherland, they had leisure and immunity enough to develop themselves physically and spiritually. To such a people the doctrine had application, and for them its significance was self-evident. Only under such conditions can a purely individualistic code of ethics succeed. Only there can there be the belief — which was the Greek belief — that the best life is the life of self-development into the perfect natural norm, the life κατὰ φύσιν.

It is important to realise how completely such an ethical principle would be misinterpreted by the people of to-day. Self-development is not self-aggrandisement. But many modern nations have lost the sense for form and substituted a sense for size. They have been rightly taunted with treating everything quantitatively, and many men to-day hold an individualistic creed which prompts them to believe that the more they have of the good things of the world, the better it is for them. Metaphorically, we have ceased to know that, though rain is good for the rose, the water-floods of Noah cannot benefit it. Nature, to attain her end, must have her necessities in right quantities. Too much is often as disastrous as too little. To develop ourselves to the perfect norm, we need, not as much of everything as possible, but just so much as is consonant with the particular demands of our particular nature.

It is easy to see that this is true of the simpler organisms such as plants and animals. Overfeeding and underfeeding are both bad because both are contrary to natural requirements, — they are παρὰ φύσιν. Both produce in the affected organism a departure from the true norm, a formal distortion, and a consequent imperfect state. It is not hard to see that, in man likewise, the physical part is in a similar condition, that under-exercise or over-eating are detrimental. Yet we now-a-days feel our impaired state of health to be a sin against good judgment rather than against morality. But the best Greeks of the Polykleitan age, with their peculiar attitude toward athletics, would have felt it to be an offence against that formal perfection of the human body which is for man the only physical state worthy of his aspiration.

Compare the Polykleitan Doryphoros with the Herakles Farnese of a later and other age. The one is physical perfection, the other is physical exaggeration. The history of early Peloponnesian sculpture is little else than the gradual evolution of the completely and harmoniously developed type of the male human body. The slow-yielding stone bears record to that incessant striving of the Greek to allow Nature her formally wonderful self-expression, which prompted him to Olympian festivals wherein the victory was not merely a glorification of muscle and sinew, but also the visible triumph of human φύσις that had realized her εἶδος.[7]

Because he was so sensitive to this formal perfection which is Nature's successful self-expression, it was apparently an inevitable consequence that the Greek applied to everything the standard of material form. He saw spiritual problems as it were from a physical point of view. Man's spiritual growth was somehow similar to that material growth whose athletic perfection the Greek so greatly loved. To one and the other, the same general laws applied. The athletic training-school reappeared as a spiritual paedeutic. Man's thinking and volitional nature must be formed by exercise into a natural state of health and strength. The sophists and rhetors were but athletic trainers in the palaestra of thought. The Greek youth learned to wrestle intellectually not primarily for display or gain, but because only so was the

[7] Euripides' polemic against athletes is in itself a protest against the professional vulgarisation of this high athletic ideal (and not against the ideal itself). (Fr. 284).

intellectual body, with all its sinews of reason and knowledge, brought
into its proper state of health. So only could the intellectual φύσις
réalise its εἶδος fully.

Compare again the Polykleitan Doryphoros and the Herakles Farnese. Think of them, however, as an allegory of man's intellectual and
spiritual self. The Doryphoros gives us the classic Greek ideal: through
self-denial if necessary, through constant energy, and unfailing self-
attention, all the spiritual powers are developed in harmony with each
other until they give the fullest expression to that balanced and perfect type toward which Nature always strives, but which she can attain
only if the individual himself will aid her. All the right conditions must
be there, before the rose at last unfolds its petals and displays the perfect flower, — a wholly natural product, this flawless plant, and yet
in nature how rare!

It is a creed which is absolutely individualistic and self-centred;
but it involves both devotion and painful energy. Selfishness and self-
aggrandisement produce a spiritual Herakles Farnese. It needs an
intense training, a deep feeling for spiritual φύσις, a sense of moderation
and restraint in mental diet and immaterial exercise, before the perfected form, the spiritual Doryphoros, can emerge. It is not a doctrine
of self-indulgence. But far less is it a doctrine of self-suppression. It
is the precise opposite: it is self-expression by unwearying attention
to the ways of that universal nature which guides plants and animals
through their wonderful growth toward that completed individual
form which they all attain in some measure, but which only those attain
fully and perfectly for whom all the conditions are right. Ethics is the
study of these conditions in the case of the human organism. The pursuit of these conditions is at once right conduct and the highest individual
good. "To live in the norm of nature is to live rightly and well":
τὸ ζῆν κατὰ φύσιν ἐστὶν εὖ ζῆν.

This general attitude toward existence was so deep-rooted in the
Greek mind that it became a unifying principle for all his ethical thought.
From it, deliberately or instinctively, he drew his moral sanction. Like
" revealed word of God," or " innate consciousness of right and wrong,"
it gave a starting-point outside of the individual and independent of
his subjective vagaries.

How thoroughly it interpenetrated Greek moral thought I intend
to show by an examination of Euripides.[8] By constant appeal to his

[8] I have thus far given no references in support of my view, because so general
an attitude must be based not merely on the whole of Greek literature, but on

dramas I hope to emphasise the fact that some of the striking differences between the Greek and Christian attitude toward moral questions are largely due to this initial divergence in the source of Moral Sanction. I wish to show how far the Euripidean ethic proves itself consistent, when once its fundamental proposition is adopted. I mean, further, to suggest that the Aristotelian ethic is largely a prose statement, helped out by a certain quantity of logical fermentation, of what the tragic stage inculcated into Athenian audiences; and that the service of Aristotle in his famous Nicomachean Ethics was not so much that of creating a system of ethics as of supplying a logical and psychological framework for an otherwise highly developed and intelligently thought-out morality. Indeed, we should expect this to be true, on the general ground that the moral philosophers are largely engaged in rationalising the convictions of their fellow-men; so that it would be strange indeed if so intellectual and so ethical a product as the Greek drama had not already uttered all the fundamental tenets of the Nicomachean Ethics. But it is one thing to suspect a truth and another thing to prove it in its specific exemplification. In the following chapters, accordingly, I have gone into the logical detail of the Euripidean ethic, championed its simplicity and its rationality, and tried to show both how highly it is developed and how little change is necessary to cast it in obvious Aristotelian form.

Greek art and life as well. Euripides himself uses the actual word φύσις sparingly, perhaps in no case in order to give expression to a definite ethical teaching. I believe that the quotations from Euripides, which follow, will give ample corroboration for this introductory chapter; but from the nature of the subject, the evidence must be cumulative rather than specific.

I might, however, refer to the extraordinary frequency with which moral evil is spoken of as disease or sickness, to show how intimately the Greek mind connected the physical and the ethical. νόσος is a violation of φύσις in its physical aspect: moral evil is a similar malady in conduct. I add a few instances of this usage. It would be easy to treble the list: Fr. 227; 294; 431; 609; Hipp. 730.

CHAPTER II

We may ask ourselves how the individual is to know this norm of nature which Greek morality bids him follow. He will know it, in outline at least, from his early training. Presupposing that his teachers already understand this norm, its principles can be firmly imbedded in his childhood mind at an age when he could otherwise have no grasp of it. Right training is thus of the greatest ethical importance, and it is not surprising to see Euripides frequently emphasising its value.

Thus Fragment 926:

> παῖς ὧν φυλάσσου πραγμάτων αἰσχρῶν ἄπο·
> ὡς ἢν τραφῇ τις μὴ κακῶς, αἰσχύνεται
> ἀνὴρ γενόμενος αἰσχρὰ δρᾶν· νέος δ' ὅταν
> πόλλ' ἐξαμάρτῃ, τὴν ἁμαρτίαν ἔχει
> εἰς γῆρας αὐτοῦ τοῖς τρόποισιν ἔμφυτον.[1]

In the Suppliants,[2] Adrastus lauds the great warriors who fell in battle before the gates of Thebes. After recounting their individual worth and valour, he praises the good training which set such courage in their souls:

> τὸ γὰρ τραφῆναι μὴ κακῶς αἰδῶ φέρει·
> αἰσχύνεται δὲ τἀγάθ' ἀσκήσας ἀνὴρ
> κακὸς γενέσθαι πᾶς τις. ἡ δ' εὐανδρία
> διδακτός, εἴπερ καὶ βρέφος διδάσκεται
> λέγειν ἀκούειν θ' ὧν μάθησιν οὐκ ἔχει.
> ἃ δ' ἂν μάθῃ τις, ταῦτα σῴζεσθαι φιλεῖ
> πρὸς γῆρας. οὕτω παῖδας εὖ παιδεύετε.
>
> (Hik. 911–17)

Hekabe, in the play of that name, remarks that the good are ever good and the bad are ever bad, and wonders to what cause this may be due:

> ἆρ' οἱ τεκόντες διαφέρουσιν ἢ τροφαί;
> ἔχει γε μέντοι καὶ τὸ θρεφθῆναι καλῶς
> δίδαξιν ἐσθλοῦ· τοῦτο δ' ἢν τις εὖ μάθῃ,
> οἶδεν τό γ' αἰσχρόν, κανόνι τοῦ καλοῦ μαθών.
>
> (Hek. 599–602)

---

[1] The extant plays are quoted from Gilbert Murray's edition, in the Oxford Classical Texts, and the Fragments from the latest Teubner text (ed. Nauck).
[2] Hik. 857–917.

10

A further instance occurs in the Iphigeneia in Aulis:

> KLYTAIMESTRA: Who trained Achilles, Thetis or his father?
> AGAMEMNON: 'Twas Cheiron lest he learn bad tricks of mortals.
> KLYTAIMESTRA: Ah, wise the trainer; but the father, wiser.
>
> (I. A. 708–10) [3]

But though for the individual this training in the norm of nature may be practicable and to a certain extent sufficient, it of course does not solve the ethical problem raised at the beginning of this chapter. How is man to learn the norm of Nature which it is his duty and highest good to follow?

The physical norm can be learned by experience and trial. The rules of the athletic training-school are empiric in their origin. The right amount of exercise, of food, of sleep, can be ascertained by experiment. The same is true of man's spiritual activities. We may violate the norm by excess or by defect; but if we are attentive to the results, we shall learn at last the due amount. The "golden mean" is thus an empiric rule. Our reason gives us merely the rule in all its generality, telling us that, since we are natural organisms, we must fit ourselves as completely as possible to Nature's requirements, and that, since we may err either by too much or by too little, our aim must be to discover the norm between excess and defect. Such advice is excellent, but not specific. In every part of conduct, in every act, we must pause and ask ourselves, "What does φύσις here require? Where is that balance between too much and too little, which is the perfect requirement and condition of Nature?"

This is the difficulty of Greek ethics. The fundamental principle must be elaborated in every part of life, in all the emotions and intellectual conditions, in every portion of the system of human conduct. Only if it can be shown to be true without exception, to be as infallible in practice as it is plausible in theory, only then can it be proclaimed a great and necessary principle of living. It is only then that we are justified in considering it as it were the ethical spine which makes a coherent and organic articulation out of what would otherwise be merely an invertebrate mass of precepts.

In the Hippolytos, Phaidra's nurse — a prosaic soul full of middle-class wisdom — appeals to the seven sages: [4]

---

[3] Cf. the chorus in the same play, ll. 561–2.
[4] If this inference to the Wise Men may be made from the collocation of the familiar μηδὲν ἄγαν and the suggestive σοφοί.

οὕτω τὸ λίαν ἧσσον ἐπαινῶ
τοῦ μηδὲν ἄγαν·
καὶ ξυμφήσουσι σοφοί μοι.

(Hipp. 264-6)

Nihil nimium (or, in Terence's phrase, *ut ne quid nimis*),[5] is a corner-
stone for conduct because:

βροτοῖς τὰ μείζω τῶν μέσων τίκτει νόσους.

(Fragment 80)

The plays, in fact, are full of warnings against excess.[6] But it is the
specific application of the general rule which Euripides never wearies
of emphasising and exemplifying. And, as we saw, an empiric rule
must offer precisely this proof in detail. I give, under various headings,
passages in Euripides to show the poet's thoroughgoing crusade for
moderation in conduct.

1. In courage and fear, the evil of excess:

μὴ τὰ κινδυνεύματα
αἰνεῖτ'· ἐγὼ γὰρ οὕτε ναυτίλον φιλῶ
τολμῶντα λίαν οὕτε προστάτην χθονός.

(Fragment 194)

τὰς τῶν θεῶν γὰρ ὅστις ἐκμοχθεῖ τύχας,
πρόθυμός ἐστιν, ἡ προθυμία δ' ἄφρων.

(H. M. 309-10)

The evil of defect:

δειλοὶ γὰρ ἄνδρες οὐκ ἔχουσιν ἐν μάχῃ
ἀριθμόν, ἀλλ' ἄπεισι κἂν παρῶσ' ὅμως.

(Fragment 523)

. . . τοὺς πόνους γὰρ ἀγαθοὶ
τολμῶσι, δειλοὶ δ' εἰσὶν οὐδὲν οὐδαμοῦ.

(I. T. 114-15)

ὁ δ' ἡδὺς αἰὼν ἡ κακή τ' ἀνανδρία
οὔτ' οἶκον οὔτε πόλιν ἀνορθώσειεν ἄν.

(Fragment 241)

Praise of the right amount of courage:

νεανίαν γὰρ ἄνδρα χρὴ τολμᾶν ἀεί·
οὐδεὶς γὰρ ὢν ῥάθυμος εὐκλεὴς ἀνήρ,
ἀλλ' οἱ πόνοι τίκτουσι τὴν εὐανδρίαν.

(Fragment 239)

[5] Andria, 61.
[6] E.g. Med. 127-8; Phoin. 539-42; 554; 584; Fr. 80; 628, l. 4; 964.

φεύγειν μὲν οὖν χρὴ πόλεμον ὅστις εὖ φρονεῖ·
εἰ δ' ἐς τόδ' ἔλθοι, στέφανος οὐκ αἰσχρὸς πόλει
καλῶς ὀλέσθαι, μὴ καλῶς δὲ δυσκλεές.[7]

(Kasandra in Tro. 400-3)

Praise of the right amount of fear:

. . . οὐκ αἰνῶ φόβον,
ὅστις φοβεῖται μὴ διεξελθὼν λόγῳ,

(Tro. 1165-6)

implying that reason should determine the due extent to which fear is justified.

2. So, in general mental and physical activity, those who are over-energetic and those who love the life of inglorious ease are both at fault. Somewhere between the two extremes runs the course of right conduct:

ὁ πλεῖστα πράσσων πλεῖσθ' ἁμαρτάνει βροτῶν.

(Fragment 580)

In the lost play Philoktetes, Odysseus speaks of his own folly in striving for cunning and wisdom beyond due measure:

πῶς δ' ἂν φρονοίην, ᾧ παρῆν ἀπραγμόνως
ἐν τοῖσι πολλοῖς ἠριθμημένῳ στρατοῦ
ἴσον μετασχεῖν τῷ σοφωτάτῳ τύχης;

(Fragment 785)

Similarly, the other extreme is wrong:

. . . τίς δ' ἄμοχθος εὐκλεής;
τίς τῶν μεγίστων δειλὸς ὢν ὠρέξατο;

(From Fragment 242)

. . . εἰ δ' ἄτερ πόνων
δοκεῖς ἔσεσθαι, μῶρος εἶ, θνητὸς γεγώς.[8]

(Fragment 396)

The right amount in energy and activity is alone right, and this is either energy as opposed to laziness:

ἐκ τῶν πόνων τοι τἀγάθ' αὔξεται βροτοῖς,

(From Fragment 366)

μοχθεῖν ἀνάγκη τοὺς θέλοντας εὐτυχεῖν,

(Fragment 719)

or else self-restraint as opposed to over-activity:

ὁ δ' ἥσυχος φίλοισί τ' ἀσφαλὴς φίλος
πόλει τ' ἄριστος. . . .[9]

(From Fragment 194)

[7] Cf. also Fr. 304; 420; 437; 745; 1038.
[8] Cf. also Fr. 241 and the almost identical lines in 366.
[9] Cf. also Fr. 235; 238; 464; 477; 745; mainly praising energy.

The apparent inconsistency in these three fragments vanishes only if
we recognise that the first two praise the mean as opposed to the defect,
while the third praises the mean as opposed to the excess.

3. The doctrine of the mean has perhaps its greatest value in man's
emotional pursuits, where pleasure and dislike are such powerful factors,
and where man is, as nowhere else, prone to rush into extremes. It is
consequently the excess rather than the defect against which man needs
warning and such passages are more numerous in Euripides than those
which emphasise the opposite extreme. And yet there is one entire play
which has this latter function to perform. I judge that with the Hippolytos Euripides is preaching as usual (but by an unusual example) his
fundamental ethical doctrine that conduct contrary to nature must end
in disaster. Hippolytos is insensible to the attraction of love, and because he thereby behaves παρά φύσιν, the φύσις which he has violated, that
same power and instinct of love, reacts against him in the person of
Phaidra and brings about his ruin and his violent death. In confirma-
tion, there is a fragment from that other and earlier play of the Veiled
Hippolytos, of which we should so gladly know more. There we read:

> οἱ γὰρ Κύπριν φεύγοντες ἀνθρώπων ἄγαν
> νοσοῦσ' ὁμοίως τοῖς ἄγαν θηρωμένοις.
>
> (Fragment 431)

The Hippolytos is such a brilliant and careful exposition of
Euripides' fundamental moral thesis that it is essential for me to ex-
amine it at greater length. The play has been very generally misappre-
hended, because the author's intentions toward Hippolytos have not
been understood. To a careful reader, who bears our moral thesis in
mind, it must be abundantly clear that Euripides is not in sympathy
with Hippolytos, but is strongly censuring an attitude which was probably prevalent in his own town of Athens and which strongly recalls
the aesthetic and other "literary" movements of the closing years of
the nineteenth century in England. From his first appearance on the
stage, a certain preciosity is noticeable in the words of Hippolytos.
He talks of flowers [10] and jewelry [11] and maintains an attitude of *odi
profanum vulgus* (from whom he is *toto caelo* distinct).[12] He belongs to
a "set" ὅσοις διδακτὸν μηδὲν ἀλλ' ἐν τῇ φύσει. (l. 79). To the last he is
exclusive, and despises the bourgeois gift of demagogic oratory:

> ἐγὼ δ' ἄκομψος εἰς ὄχλον δοῦναι λόγον,
> ἐς ἥλικας δὲ κὠλίγους σοφώτερος.
>
> (*ib.* 986–7)

[10] Hipp. 73–8.   [11] *Ib.* 82–3.   [12] *Ib.* 79–81; 84.

He is of the *jeunesse dorée* who spend time on horses and hunting. These
very horses cause his undoing. In ancient tragedy the agents of disaster
are chosen with grim appropriateness. ἀκήρατος, " unsullied," is a favourite word of his.[13] It has a self-righteous ring, a note of moral arrogance,
ὕβρις. It turns to injured innocence in ll. 654–6 where he spurns the
suggestions of the old nurse, and shows a complete lack of sympathy.
He is inhuman in his ἀναισθησία. Just this quality in him spurs Phaidra
to her fatal actions. Bitterly she says, "that he may learn not to be
high and mighty about my misfortune" (ἵν᾿ εἰδῇ μὴ 'πὶ τοῖς ἐμοῖς κακοῖς
ὑψηλὸς εἶναι).[14]

From his father Theseus we have further light on Hippolytos, who
is taunted with a bitter reference to his reputation as a superman of
refinement (περισσὸς ἀνήρ).[15] ἀκήρατος, "unsullied," his favourite word,
is hurled in his face.[16] Apparently Theseus has found his son's affec-
tations (κόμποι) hard to endure. He has had to put up with his vege-
tarianism, religious mysticism, and literary dilettanteism.[17] His whole
speech is the reaction of the normal man against the abnormal. Theseus
is healthy in mind and body; Hippolytos seems to be neither. It is
the clash of τὰ κατὰ φύσιν with τὰ παρὰ φύσιν, and the latter must go
under. Lest the spectator think that the approaching catastrophe is
accidental or individual, due to casual misunderstanding or spite or
sudden rage, Euripides makes Theseus declare the universality of his
attitude. It is not Theseus against Hippolytos, it is the natural
against the abnormal:

<blockquote>
τοὺς δὲ τοιούτους ἐγὼ
φεύγειν προφωνῶ πᾶσι·

(955–6)
</blockquote>

τοιούτους and πᾶσι are no longer specific or personal terms.

Hippolytos defends himself against his father's charges in a speech
betraying affectation and self-righteousness.[18] He is σώφρων,[19] without
sexual interest,[20] a virgin.[21]

<blockquote>
οἴμοι, τὸ σεμνὸν ὥς μ᾿ ἀποκτενεῖ τὸ σόν.
Oh, how thy holy cant will murder me!
</blockquote>

cries Theseus.[22] The same τὸ σεμνόν is one cause of Hippolytos' undoing. He was warned against it at the opening of the play by his huntsman.[23] But it is ἐν τῇ φύσει. Even when near death, he clings to his

---

[13] Hipp. 73, 76; cf. 949.   [15] Ib. 948.   [17] Ib. 952–4.   [19] Ib. 995.
[14] Ib. 729–30.   [16] Ib. 949.   [18] Ib. 983 ff.   [20] Ib. 1006.
[21] ἄθικτος, 1002. But it must be granted that his ideal in 1016–8 is both a healthy
and a good one.   [22] Ib. 1064.   [23] Ib. 91–5.

σεμνὸς ἐγώ.[24] But the last scene is one of reconciliation. Sympathy with his father breaks his σεμνότης.[25] In his last words, he becomes at last natural and human. He turns against his old life as personified in Artemis. (In 1441-3 does he not even seem to suggest that he finds her a trifle verbose and tedious?) φύσις has reclaimed him, and Theseus, the normal man, weeps for his dying son.

Of all Hippolytos' abnormalities, however, the most fatal was his complete aversion to love. Aphrodite, speaking the prologue and explaining the argument, announced the unvengeful and almost impersonal retribution of this slighted instinct,[26] and Phaidra is declared the unwitting victim of the reaction.[27] The huntsman warns Hippolytos of this force which he spurns;[28] but without effect. Straightway thereafter, love asserts itself in Phaidra's unhappy struggle.

With the appearance of Theseus, we realize that slighted love has fulfilled its terrible reaction. And now the other charges of abnormality are developed against Hippolytos, as explained above. But observe that after the death of Hippolytos, when Theseus and Poseidon are alone vivid in the spectator's thoughts, the chorus without a word of transition harks back to Aphrodite to whom all this tragedy is ascribed.[29] The mangled Hippolytos is brought upon the stage. He is still unrepentant. When disaster overtook him, amid the turmoil of broken wheel and dragging rein, he called himself still "a perfect man" (ἀνδρ' ἄριστον, 1242). And now he ascribes his misfortune to inherited guilt.[30] But Artemis tells him the true cause,[31] and Theseus, who closes the play, attributes all to Kypris, the power of love.[32]

It is a grim spectacle, because all the characters are merely puppets playing the great but unequal game of φύσις against τὸ παρὰ φύσιν. But just because it is so universal, it is true tragedy and true morality. That morality is Greek to the core.

The Medeia illustrates the opposite extreme. Princess of the royal blood of Kolchis, she deserted her land and slew her brother, for love of a foreign adventurer. Bitterly she exclaims to Jason, "To my friends at home I made myself a foe, and those whom ne'er I should have wronged, for the sake of you I made my enemies!"[33] Endowed with strange knowledge, a creature with the sun-god's passion in her veins and sister to the enchantress Kirke, she sacrificed everything for love.

[24] Hipp. 1364.   [28] Ib. 88-120.   [31] Ib. 1400 and 1402.
[25] Ib. 1405-15.   [29] Ib. 1268-82.   [32] Ib. 1461.
[26] Ib. 20-22.   [30] Ib. 1379 ff.   [33] Med. 506-8.
[27] Ib. 27-28; cf. 47-50.

Outraging Nature, she falls a victim to Nature's recoil. Her wild love turns into barbaric hate. She slaughters her own children, and vanishes. The chariot of dragons, on which she disappears, is not more strange than she to Nature's normal ways.[34]

4. Passages against excess in pleasure are numerous in Euripides:

> . . . ἡ φύσις γὰρ οἴχεται
> ὅταν γλυκείας ἡδονῆς ἥσσων τις ᾖ.
>
> (From Fragment 187)

> τὰ χρήστ' ἐπιστάμεσθα καὶ γιγνώσκομεν,
> οὐκ ἐκπονοῦμεν δ', οἱ μὲν ἀργίας ὕπο,
> οἱ δ' ἡδονὴν προθέντες ἀντὶ τοῦ καλοῦ
> ἄλλην τιν'.
>
> (Hipp. 380–3)

> ὅταν κακοὶ πράξωσιν, ὦ ξένοι, καλῶς,
> ἄγαν κρατοῦντες κοὐ νομίζοντες δίκην
> δώσειν ἔδρασαν πάντ' ἐφέντες ἡδονῇ.[35]
>
> (Fragment 568)

But though pleasure with its irrational power is in general a danger, it is not in itself an evil if man can only enjoy within due bounds. In this the Greek differs from much mediaeval Christian doctrine and displays an attitude more akin to the modern. With our thought coloured by evolutional and biological theory, we judge pleasure as a natural appearance, valuable and necessary for man's maintenance. In just the same way the Greek saw pleasure to be "according to nature," a normal and admirable product. The ideal was not to avoid pleasure, but to learn how to use it. There is a remark made by Pylades in the Iphigeneia in Tauris which may be elevated to a general gnome of this Greek attitude toward pleasure: .

> σοφῶν γὰρ ἀνδρῶν ταῦτα, μὴ 'κβάντας τύχης,
> καιρὸν λαβόντας, ἡδονὰς ἄλλας λαβεῖν.[36]
>
> (I. T. 907–8)

[34] Perhaps also (as Prof. H. N. Sanders has pointed out to me) the play is a veiled protest against the legitimation and naturalisation of the children which Perikles had by Aspasia. In that case the appeal is similarly to the plea of παρὰ φύσιν, under whose ban legalised international marriage is easily made to fall.

[35] Cf. also Fragments 197; 364 (ll. 22–23); 849.

[36] ἄλλας in the Greek idiom is attracted to ἡδονάς. It does not mean "other pleasures," but "other things, which are pleasures." So in Hipp. 383, just above.

Similarly:

> τὸ δ' ἐρᾶν προλέγω τοῖσι νέοισιν
> μήποτε φεύγειν,
> χρῆσθαι δ' ὀρθῶς ὅταν ἔλθῃ,

(From Fragment 889)

which, as we have seen, is very much the moral of the entire Hippolytos.

The self-control which never runs into excess of pleasure is known in Greek as sophrosyne. It does not mean abstinence or asceticism, but the ability to maintain the mean amid temptations to excess. Consequently it most frequently has reference to pleasure. But sophrosyne is not mere negative restraint. To understand it, we must read the Bacchae, a play of first importance for our thesis. I can see no sign that the drama is the palinode of an atheist or the apologia of a rationalist,[37] an old man in exile trying to reconcile himself with popular religion. The "orthodox" view seems obviously correct; for Euripides' own words are insistent in its favour. It is nearly the same subject as in the Hippolytos: the Bacchic pleasures and prerogatives — dancing, laughter, freedom from care, wine-feasting[38] — are natural and salutary. To treat them with austerity and suppression is therefore not virtue, but a violation of nature, and quite strictly παρὰ φύσιν. Hence the fateful recoil of these Bacchic elements of life on Pentheus, even as love recoiled to work the death of Hippolytos. More than this, man's φύσις includes more than a mere life of reason. All that fine intoxication of the spirit, with which poet and votary are so familiar, is not outside of Nature's intent. Euripides would have been turning a weapon against himself, were he to admit that poetic enthusiasm is παρὰ φύσιν. Rather, its suppression and denial are παρὰ φύσιν, and baleful. Let us be poets and Bacchants, since we have it in us! Enjoyed in right amount, Dionysos is κατὰ φύσιν and a moral necessity, very different from excess or licentiousness as the chorus is careful to point out.[39] Nor is it true that his rites lead necessarily to dissipation:

> οὐχ ὁ Διόνυσος σωφρονεῖν ἀναγκάσει
> γυναῖκας ἐς τὴν Κύπριν, ἀλλ' ἐν τῇ φύσει
> [τὸ σωφρονεῖν ἔνεστιν εἰς τὰ πάντ' ἀεί][40]

---

[37] As, among others, Sir John Sandys would have us believe in his edition of the play (Cambridge, 1900, Introd. lxxv).

[38] All these enumerated o. c. 379–85.

[39] Ib. 386–8.

[40] Ib. 314–6.

The chorus states the whole matter admirably:

> τιμῶν τε Βρόμιον σωφρονεῖς.
> "Give Dionysos his due, and you will be σώφρων." [41]

Sophrosyne is not abstinence, but proper acquiescence in Nature's ways. The Hippolytos takes pains to illustrate the true meaning of the word. Hippolytos is fond of calling himself σώφρων [42] and Artemis agrees with his definition.[43] But Phaidra has a different conception of sophrosyne:

> ἀτὰρ κακόν γε χἀτέρῳ γενήσομαι
> θανοῦσ', ἵν' εἰδῇ μὴ 'πὶ τοῖς ἐμοῖς κακοῖς
> ὑψηλὸς εἶναι. τῆς νόσου δὲ τῆσδέ μοι
> κοινῇ μετασχὼν σωφρονεῖν μαθήσεται.

> (Hipp. 728–31)

Which definition of sophrosyne has the poet's own approval, we may read writ large through all the play.

We should remember that because the Greeks, like most southern races, were inclined to excess, restraint was to them an inherent part of conduct. Where northern peoples are apt to phrase the ethical alternative as "to do or not to do," and make a sheer choice between extreme poles, the southern shift the problem to the intermediary zones and make the choice one of degree. The Corcyra massacres in Thucydides are an instance of the excess into which the Greek was not infrequently betrayed. Alexandrianism and Byzantinism show the ultimate assertion of these fervid tendencies which, in the preceding classical age, were controlled only by the most constant application. Indeed, one may suspect that Greek art and literature show essentially the curbs and checks of a conscious formalism trying to hold in restraint the dithyrambic excess of the national temperament. By having, in general, only the formal product preserved to us, we miss the ever-present contrast with the unrestrained world with which they struggled.[44] Only on such a supposition can we understand why the doctrine of the Mean forms such an apparently disproportionate part of Aristotle's Ethics and why Euripides could write whole plays

---

[41] *Ib.* 329.   [42] E.g. 80, 1365.   [43] *Ib.* 1402.

[44] The terra cotta figurines often echo the popular temperament unrestrained by artistic formalisation. Cf. the well-known caricatures mostly found in Asia Minor, and monstrosities such as were discovered in the Demeter sanctuary at Priene, illustrated in Wiegand-Schrader's *Priene.*

primarily to exemplify the value and necessity of harmonious and balanced conduct.

The references have emphasized that in love, even more than elsewhere, the need of moderation obtains.   The following passages are equally illustrative of this teaching: [45]

ἔρωτες ὑπὲρ μὲν ἄγαν
ἐλθόντες οὐκ εὐδοξίαν
οὐδ' ἀρετὰν παρέδωκαν
ἀνδράσιν· εἰ δ' ἅλις ἔλθοι
Κύπρις, οὐκ ἄλλα θεὸς εὔχαρις οὕτως.
(Chorus, Med. 627–31)

μάκαρες οἱ μετρίας θεοῦ
μετά τε σωφροσύνας μετέ-
σχον λέκτρων 'Αφροδίτας,
γαλανείᾳ χρησάμενοι
μανιάδων οἴστρων, ὅθι δὴ
δίδυμ' Ἔρως ὁ χρυσοκόμας
τόξ' ἐντείνεται χαρίτων,
τὸ μὲν ἐπ' εὐαίωνι πότμῳ,
τὸ δ' ἐπὶ συγχύσει βιοτᾶς.
.   .   .   .
εἴη δέ μοι μετρία μὲν
χάρις, πόθοι δ' ὅσιοι,
καὶ μετέχοιμι τᾶς 'Αφροδίτας, πολλὰν δ' ἀποθείμαν.
(Chorus, I. A. 543–51; 554–7)

μετρίων λέκτρων, μετρίων δὲ γάμων
μετὰ σωφροσύνης
κῦρσαι θνητοῖσιν ἄριστον.
(Fragment 505)

Finally there is the praise of love in a fragment of eleven lines ascribed to Euripides:

παίδευμα δ' Ἔρως σοφίας ἀρετῆς
πλεῖστον ὑπάρχει,
καὶ προσομιλεῖν οὗτος ὁ δαίμων
πάντων ἥδιστος ἔφυ θνητοῖς.

[45] Cf. similarly, Hipp. 358; 431–2; also Fragment 449 from the earlier Hippolytos; Fr. 507; 951; Med. 635–6.

καὶ γὰρ ἄλυπον τέρψιν τιν' ἔχων
εἰς ἐλπίδ' ἄγει. τοῖς δ' ἀτελέστοις
τῶν τοῦδε πόνων μήτε συνείην
χωρὶς τ' ἀγρίων ναίοιμι τρόπων.
τὸ δ' ἐρᾶν προλέγω τοῖσι νέοισιν
μήποτε φεύγειν,
χρῆσθαι δ' ὀρθῶς, ὅταν ἔλθῃ.

(Fragment 889)

5. Similarly, the rest of man's emotions are not to be frowned upon nor treated with the unrecognising stare of a merciless self-suppression. The emotions are natural products. To deny them their due place in man's life is to attain, not a higher ethical plane, but an unhuman one. The problem of the individual is not to avoid emotion, but to avoid, now excessive emotionality, now emotional insensibility. For example, although indulgence in anger is generally injurious to men, there are instances where a lack of resentment proclaims a spiritless creature, a thing somewhat less than a man, like that Phrygian slave in the latter part of the Orestes (ll. 1369 ff.) whose barbaric panic and cringing submission fill us with contempt. Not to harbour just anger and desire for revenge is, in fact, characteristic of the serf; and, in Greek thought, the barbarian slave who behaves as a slave, is of a lower and different order than real man.[46] The free-born Greek had a duty toward his own self-respect. Ἐλευθερότης, the conduct of individual independence, was part of his φύσις. Not to maintain it was παρὰ φύσιν and ethically wrong. With just this plea Orestes announces his vengeance against Menelaos:

δράσας τι χρῄζω τοὺς ἐμοὺς ἐχθροὺς θανεῖν,
ἵν' ἀνταναλώσω μὲν οἵ με προύδοσαν,
στένωσι δ' οἵπερ κἄμ' ἔθηκαν ἄθλιον.
Ἀγαμέμνονός τοι παῖς πέφυχ' . . .
. . . . ὃν οὐ καταισχυνῶ
δοῦλον παρασχὼν θάνατον, ἀλλ' ἐλευθέρως
ψυχὴν ἀφήσω, Μενέλεων δὲ τείσομαι.

(Or. 1164–7; 1169–71)

Though the evil of excessive anger is often emphasised in Euripides, — as for example in the following,

πολλοὺς δ' ὁ θυμὸς ὁ μέγας ὤλεσεν βροτῶν

(Fragment 259)

[46] Cf. Fr. 215.

ὀργῇ γὰρ ὅστις εὐθέως χαρίζεται
κακῶς τελευτᾷ. . .⁴⁷

(Fragment 31)

none the less, there is such a thing as justifiable anger, —

γέροντες, αἰνῶ· τῶν φίλων γὰρ οὕνεκα
ὀργὰς δικαίας τοὺς φίλους ἔχειν χρεών,

(H. M. 275-6)

and in the Herakleidai, when Alkmene at last holds her implacable enemy Eurystheus in her power and claims that her right of vengeance is greater than the laws of Marathon, the chorus calls her rage συγγνωστόν, "comprehensible," and so "pardonable."⁴⁸ In another play, where Hekabe takes a hideous revenge on Polymestor for the violation of the sanctity of hospitality and the murder of her son, Agamemnon, in true Euripidean fashion, holds an ethical inquest and justifies Hekabe for blinding Polymestor. The decision gains weight, because awarded by a Greek against an ally and in favour of a hereditary foe.⁴⁹

In fact, where resentment is justified, it is mere weakness to indulge the opposite emotional extreme. Forgiveness and compassion may be as wrong and disastrous as wrathful implacability. Though a Fragment bids:

. . . μὴ σκυθρωπὸς ἴσθ' ἄγαν
πρὸς τοὺς κακῶς πράσσοντας, ἄνθρωπος γεγώς,

(Fragment 410)

yet, in the Medeia, Kreon by yielding to his pity for the woman whose viperous hate and cunning he secretly dreads and understands, exposes himself to vengeance at her hands. He acknowledges his error even while he commits it:

αἰδούμενος δὲ πολλὰ δὴ διέφθορα·
καὶ νῦν ὁρῶ μὲν ἐξαμαρτάνων, γύναι,
ὅμως δὲ τεύξῃ τοῦδε·

(Med. 349-51)

Scarcely has Kreon left the stage when Medeia speaks contemptuously of his unwise generosity toward her as "senseless folly."⁵⁰ It is true Greek ethic (and good logic) to despise in a foe the weakness by which one profits.

Right conduct, here as elsewhere, lies between the two extremes.

---

⁴⁷ Cf. also Fr. 760 and 796.   ⁴⁹ Hek. 1129-1251.
⁴⁸ Herakl. 981.   ⁵⁰ Med. 371 ff.

Anger must be justified by reason, for reason alone can divine the proper norm. Medeia, in yielding wholly to her passion and rage, realises that anger in her has exceeded its proper function and that she is morally at fault:

καὶ μανθάνω μὲν οἶα δρᾶν μέλλω κακά,
θυμὸς δὲ κρείσσων τῶν ἐμῶν βουλευμάτων,
ὅσπερ μεγίστων αἴτιος κακῶν βροτοῖς.

(Med. 1078-80)

Two fragments present the same doctrine:

ὥρα σε θυμοῦ κρείσσονα γνώμην ἔχειν.

(Fragment 715)

πόλλ' ἐστὶν ὀργῆς ἐξ ἀπαιδεύτου κακά.

(Stob. Flor. 20, 12. Presumably from Euripides)

" Not too much, yet not too little." It is this that makes right conduct so rare and so difficult. For the doctrine of the mean applies to all conduct, and it is our moral duty to observe the limits between excess and defect in all that we do.

6. Even love of life, it would seem, can be carried to excess. As in all other phases of human conduct, there is a mean which alone is the right and adequate action. The defect is a form of cowardice. Herakles, when about to commit suicide from despair, checks himself with the reflection that the coward thinks death easier than misfortune: the brave man holds more fast to life.[51] Yet the other extreme is no less cowardly. Iphigeneia, before she makes her resolve to die for Greece, has gone to such excess. It is possible λίαν φιλοψυχεῖν, to love one's own life overmuch, as she herself realises.[52] Old men, says Iphis in the Hiketides,[53] cling to their useless shred of life beyond its worth. And Pheres in the Alkestis is taunted by his own son for hoarding with selfish greed the few years that yet remain before death.[54]

. It is a Greek tenet that death is better than disgrace:

. . . ἡ γὰρ αἰσχύνη πάρος
τοῦ ζῆν παρ' ἐσθλοῖς ἀνδράσιν νομίζεται.

(Herakl. 200-1)

Brave men reckon honour before life; in the choice of evils between disgrace and death it is preferable to die.[55]

[51] H. M. 1347 ff.   [53] Hik. 1108-13.
[52] I. A. 1385.   [54] Alk. 642-50 et al.
[55] Cf. H. M. 284-92; Hipp. 400-2; 426-7; Fr. 599.

7. In pleasure and pain,[56] then, in joy and grief,[57] in praise and envy,[58] in courage and fear,[59] in anger and humility,[60] in pity and compassion,[61] in friendship,[62] — in short, in all our emotional relations, Euripides exhibits to us how excess will do harm and lead man astray, while deficient sentiment will leave him too colourless and inactive, a creature below the level of that true moral agent which it is man's proper function to be.

8. But there is a large class of material and spiritual possessions, which mankind calls "the good things of this earth," against which the Few have ever preached without ever signally persuading the Many. Wealth and honour and power are good to have; and, thinks the world, the more of them one has, the better. It has always been difficult to expose the fallacy in this seemingly self-evident equation and to show that More Good does not necessarily spell Better. Greed of wealth and greed of power have been combated in many ways, — though for only one reason: because they threaten the moral equipoise of society. Moralists have cudgelled their brains to discover plausible arguments against them; obviously, as they are not at all good for *others*, the individual must be convinced that they are really not good for *him*. To produce this conviction is the aim of Plato's Republic. Of the host of other attempts, utilitarianism is perhaps the most hypocritical, as Christianity is the most sincere. What attempt at proof is there in Euripides?

Several passages praise wealth without reserve.[63] As they are all fragments and tell us neither character nor context, they are not evidence with direct bearing.[64] Had the following verses, for example, survived to us without further information than that they were from Euripides:

ὁ πλοῦτος, ἀνθρωπίσκε, τοῖς σοφοῖς θεός,
τὰ δ' ἄλλα κόμποι καὶ λόγων εὐμορφίαι,

> Mannikin! wealth the wise man's god is,
> Everything else a wordy fraud is![65]

[56] Above, pp. 14–19.
[57] Fr. 364, ll. 32–34; Herakl. 619–20; Fr. 422.
[58] Or. 1161; Fr. 297.   [59] Above, pp. 12–13.   [60] *Ib.*, pp. 21–3.   [61] *Ib.*, p. 22.
[62] Hipp. 253–60.   [63] Fr. 96; 143; 326; 327; 328; 379; 584.
[64] And here I take the opportunity to acknowledge freely the fallacy of taking every stray word as a reflection of Euripides' own convictions. There is a very real difficulty in distinguishing, in the work of a dramatic poet, what is said out of dramatic fitness from what is meant as the poet's own opinion; but in every case I have tried to base important steps in my argument on only such statements as seem to reflect Euripides *in propria persona*. Cf. the remarks of Decharme, *Euripide et l'Esprit de son Théâtre*, pp. 27–8; and also *supra*, pp. 3–4..   [65] Kykl. 316–17.

we might be puzzled what conclusions to draw. How differently we treat the passage when we learn that it is an utterance of that mighty hedonist, the Kyklops, whose high god is his belly,[66] and for whom food and warmth and sleep and animal-like irresponsibility complete the pantheon![67]

Of the fragments which praise wealth, three of the most laudatory appear to come from the lost play, Danae. A story, told by Seneca in reference to one of these three, warns us how we ought to interpret other fragments inconsonant with the attitude of Euripides in his preserved plays. In Epist. 115, Seneca gives a Latin version of Fragment 326 with its exorbitant praise of gold:

$$\mathring{\omega} \; \chi\rho\upsilon\sigma\acute{\epsilon}, \; \delta\epsilon\xi\acute{\iota}\omega\mu\alpha \; \kappa\acute{\alpha}\lambda\lambda\iota\sigma\pi\sigma\nu \; \beta\rho\sigma\tau\sigma\hat{\iota}\varsigma,$$
$$\mathring{\omega}\varsigma \; \sigma\mathring{\upsilon}\tau\epsilon \; \mu\acute{\eta}\tau\eta\rho \; \mathring{\eta}\delta\sigma\nu\grave{\alpha}\varsigma \; \tau\sigma\iota\acute{\alpha}\sigma\delta' \; \mathring{\epsilon}\chi\epsilon\iota,$$
$$\sigma\mathring{\upsilon} \; \pi\alpha\hat{\iota}\delta\epsilon\varsigma \; \mathring{\alpha}\nu\theta\rho\acute{\omega}\pi\sigma\iota\sigma\iota\nu, \; \sigma\mathring{\upsilon} \; \phi\acute{\iota}\lambda\sigma\varsigma \; \pi\alpha\tau\acute{\eta}\rho \; . \; . \; .$$
$$\epsilon\mathring{\iota} \; \delta' \; \mathring{\eta} \; K\acute{\upsilon}\pi\rho\iota\varsigma \; \tau\sigma\iota\sigma\hat{\upsilon}\tau\sigma\nu \; \mathring{\sigma}\phi\theta\alpha\lambda\mu\sigma\hat{\iota}\varsigma \; \mathring{\sigma}\rho\hat{\alpha}(\nu) \; [68]$$
$$\sigma\mathring{\upsilon} \; \theta\alpha\hat{\upsilon}\mu' \; \mathring{\epsilon}\rho\omega\tau\alpha\varsigma \; \mu\upsilon\rho\acute{\iota}\sigma\upsilon\varsigma \; \alpha\mathring{\upsilon}\tau\grave{\eta}\nu \; \mathring{\epsilon}\chi\epsilon\iota\nu,$$

(Fragment 326)

and continues, "When these verses were spoken for the first time in Euripides' tragedy, the entire audience sprang up as by a single impulse to eject both actor and play, until Euripides himself stood up in their midst and begged them to wait and see what happened to this person who thought so much of gold." We may believe the anecdote or not. Yet, with more of the context preserved, we well might see a similar fate overtake the characters in the five other fragments which praise the power and glory of wealth. At any rate, it is fairly obvious what Euripides thought on the subject. A fragment from the Alexandros[69] sounds like a taunt against Paris himself: "Wealth and luxury are an unmanly training. Poverty, though a harsh teacher, is a good one." In other Fragments, we hear that wealth dulls the sensibilities,[70] that the rich are dull in body and in mind,[71] and that wealth without intelligence is useless.[72] Riches wrongly acquired are even worse than useless,[73] for the prosperity which they bring is transient.[74] Worst of all, wealth breeds a certain $\mathring{\upsilon}\beta\rho\iota\varsigma$,[75] and therein lurks the beginning of ruin.[76]

[66] Kykl. 335.   [67] *Ib.* 323–41.
[68] Conjecturing $\mathring{\sigma}\rho\hat{\alpha}\nu$ to be Seneca's reading.
[69] Fr. 55.   [72] *Ib.* 163; 237; 1054.   [75] *Ib.* 441.
[70] *Ib.* 773.   [73] *Ib.* 822.   [76] *Ib.* 1027.
[71] *Ib.* 773; 642.   [74] *Ib.* 364, ll. 11–13; 421.

The preserved plays are better evidence for Euripides' own feeling.
The Hekabe is devoted to the punishment of avarice. Vengeance comes
at the hands of the helpless woman who has most been wronged. We
call such a dénouement "poetic" justice, implying that it scarcely
could occur in the real world of prose. Euripides, I hope to show, felt
otherwise about the matter. Again, in the play of the Suppliant Women,
Theseus characterises the march of the seven warriors against Thebes
as an example of ruin brought on by greed of honour, of power, and of
gain.[77] Later in the play, Adrastos delivers a long eulogy on the slain
seven. Concerning Tydeus he says:

> φιλότιμον ἦθος πλούσιον, φρόνημα δὲ
> ἐν τοῖσιν ἔργοις, οὐχὶ τοῖς λόγοις, ἴσον.
>
> (Hik. 907–8)

His praise of Kapaneus is still more significant:

> Καπανεὺς ὅδ᾽ ἐστίν· ᾧ βίος μὲν ἦν πολύς,
> ἥκιστα δ᾽ ὄλβῳ γαῦρος ἦν. φρόνημα δὲ
> οὐδέν τι μεῖζον εἶχεν ἢ πένης ἀνήρ.
>
> (Hik. 861–3)

Adrastos and Theseus, then, disagree in their judgment on these men.
But in one thing they seem to agree thoroughly, and that is in their
belief that too much wealth or honour bring disaster, and that only
by humility, by acting as if one had neither honours nor wealth, is it
possible to avoid destruction. The clearest expression of this belief is
in a Fragment:

> ὅταν δ᾽ ἴδῃς πρὸς ὕψος ἠρμένον τινὰ
> λαμπρῷ τε πλούτῳ καὶ γένει γαυρούμενον
> ὀφρύν τε μείζω τῆς τύχης ἐπηρκότα,
> τούτου ταχεῖαν νέμεσιν εὐθὺς προσδόκα.
>
> (Fragment 1027)

These verses sound a key-note of the histories of Herodotus and the
tetralogies of the Aeschylean drama. Euripides was an innovator: he
brought tragedy down from its ancient exalted severity, its σεμνότης,
and filled it with clever wrangle of disputes caught from law-trials and
the sophists' corner. But he never tried to rid the Attic stage of its
faith in that poetic justice which overtakes the rich and the powerful
when they presume on their high fortune. On the contrary, he keeps
displaying the power of this invisible requital; for it is a foundation-

---

[77] Hik. 232–7.

stone of his ethic. For him it is the one proof that in the "good things of this earth," in gold, in honour, and in power, there is a mean of right conduct, and an ever-present possibility of excess.

In the Herakleidai, Iolaos, an old and feeble man, suddenly displays an inexplicable folly by demanding to be armed and led into battle. Judging him for what he seems, the audience may admire, but cannot commend, his mad ambition. But later we hear, through a messenger, of wonderful feats of arms. Iolaos, the decrepit and helpless, regains his youth and strength on the field of battle[78] and takes captive Eurystheus, who, with implacable persecution of Heracles and all his race, has so long hounded that hero's ancient comrade. The play is entirely devoted to the fall of presumptuous evil-doing and the ultimate happiness of the innocent, through the liberation of the Herakleidai from the persecution of Eurystheus and their restoration to the kingship which is theirs by right. Iolaos is the sudden and miraculous embodiment of this divine retribution. As if to emphasise its unearthly origin, it incarnates itself in an outworn warrior who is unable to carry his own armour.

This is perhaps the extreme case of *justitia ex machina*. In other plays it takes a less miraculous course; but everywhere we are made to realise that something more than human agency is at work. So, in the Hekabe, the gauntlet is thrown down in challenge to heaven. Talthybios, the Greek herald, on seeing the former queen of Troy now a slave in the Greek camp, overwhelmed with misfortune, prostrate on the ground with grief, exclaims over her:

> ὦ Ζεῦ, τί λέξω; πότερά σ' ἀνθρώπους ὁρᾶν;
> ἢ δόξαν ἄλλως τήνδε κεκτῆσθαι μάτην,
> τύχην δὲ πάντα τὰν βροτοῖς ἐπισκοπεῖν;
>
> (Hek. 488–91)

Still more explicitly, Hekabe herself states the challenge:

> ἡμεῖς μὲν οὖν δοῦλοί τε κἀσθενεῖς ἴσως·
> ἀλλ' οἱ θεοὶ σθένουσι χὠ κείνων κρατῶν
> Νόμος· νόμῳ γὰρ τοὺς θεοὺς ἡγούμεθα
> καὶ ζῶμεν ἄδικα καὶ δίκαι' ὡρισμένοι·
> ὃς ἐς σ' ἀνελθὼν εἰ διαφθαρήσεται,
> καὶ μὴ δίκην δώσουσιν οἵτινες ξένους
> κτείνουσιν ἢ θεῶν ἱερὰ τολμῶσιν φέρειν,
> οὐκ ἔστιν οὐδὲν τῶν ἐν ἀνθρώποις ἴσον.
>
> (Hek. 798–805)

[78] Herakl. 843–63.

In the end, divine justice fulfils itself. The fatal avarice of Polymestor leads him into Hekabe's power. She herself accomplishes her revenge.

In the Suppliants, Theseus punishes Thebes for insolently refusing to allow burial to the slain Argive Seven. The chorus considers this intimation of justice to be a proof of the existence of a divine ordinance in the world.[79]

The plays of the Euripidean "Oresteia" are the best example of this faith in the certainty of ultimate justice. In the Aulic Iphigeneia, Agamemnon through cowardice agrees to sacrifice his daughter. Ten years later, on his return from Troy, he pays the penalty at the hands of his wife Klytaimestra. She however acted, not so much to avenge her daughter, as to cover her adultery. She has done evil, therefore, and must pay the penalty at the hands of Orestes.[80] Aigisthos, too, must suffer for his adultery and his participation in Agamemnon's death. Over his dead body, Elektra speaks the splendid lines which are a summary of all that Euripides is trying to establish:

$$\mu\acute{\eta} \ \mu οι \ τ\grave{ο} \ πρ\hat{ω}τον \ β\hat{\eta}μ' \ \grave{ε}\grave{α}ν \ δρ\acute{α}μ\eta \ καλ\hat{ω}s,$$
$$νικ\hat{α}ν \ δοκε\acuteίτω \ τ\grave{\eta}ν \ Δ\acuteίκην, \ πρ\grave{ι}ν \ \grave{α}ν \ π\acuteέλαs$$
$$γραμμ\hat{\eta}s \ \acuteίκηται \ κα\grave{ι} \ τ\acuteέλοs \ κ\acuteάμψ\eta \ β\acuteίου.$$

(El. 954–6)

In no instance can wickedness go for ever unpunished.[81] Appearances often point another way; but, in the end, justice through unknown ways fulfils herself on man. Euripides is never tired of emphasising this essential part of his faith. Thus we read that no unjust man ever prospered [82] and that in vain the wicked hope to escape.[83] The last lines of the Ion are the seal of his doctrine: [84]

$$\grave{ε}s \ τ\acuteέλοs \ γ\grave{α}ρ \ ο\grave{ι} \ μ\grave{ε}ν \ \grave{ε}σθλο\grave{ι} \ τυγχ\acuteάνουσιν \ \grave{α}ξ\acuteίων,$$
$$ο\grave{ι} \ κακο\grave{ι} \ δ', \ \grave{ω}σπερ \ πεφ\acuteύκασ', \ ο\grave{υ}ποτ' \ ε\grave{υ} \ πρ\acuteάξειαν \ \grave{α}ν.$$

(Ion 1621–2)

---

[79] Hik. 731–3.

[80] Orestes, acting purely through vengeance, seeks to fulfil justice. The death of Klytaimestra is just, but agent and means are wrong (cf. Or. 492–506). Hence Orestes too must suffer; but, because he has intended justice, he will find ultimate acquittal.

[81] In the Andromache, Menelaos ruthlessly breaks his faith, and the helpless Andromache has no weapon save her belief that the gods punish evil and maintain justice. Curiously enough, the efficacy of divine justice is never put to the test, since Peleus intervenes. This play, however, seems to be largely a loose series of events calculated to discredit Spartan character to the Athenian audience.

[82] Hel. 1030–1; cf. Fr. 646.   [84] Similarly, Fr. 224 and 559.

[83] Fr. 257; 832; cf. Hek. 1192–4.

Time will tell; [85] for it holds up a mirror to mankind, as to a young maiden's beauty,[86] and men's characters stand revealed. Time measures with a just rule,[87] and by it we know the good man from the wicked.[88]

Toward the close of the Ion, Athena says:

$$\text{ἀεὶ γὰρ οὖν}$$
$$\text{χρόνια μὲν τὰ τῶν θεῶν πως, ἐς τέλος δ' οὐκ ἀσθενῆ.}$$

(Ion 1614–5)

And this we might almost translate with the truly Greek lines:

"Though the mills of the gods grind slowly,
Yet they grind exceeding small."

With this belief that there is an unseen divine vengeance on all evil-doing, the last doubt vanishes and we understand how it is that, even when excess seems profitable to the individual, it cannot prove to be so for very long. The norm of human living is a demand of φύσις, of universal nature. If φύσις does not immediately and openly punish its violation, then slowly and invisibly she prepares the downfall of the offending individual.

Thus, Nemesis completes the proof of the doctrine of the Mean. The unseen ordinance of the world is such that it will not tolerate excess in any form. For, all excess is synonymous with a violation of φύσις; and φύσις, in one form or another, punishes τὰ παρὰ φύσιν.

The evidence which has been given is now sufficiently complete for the construction of a logical outline which will be at once a summary of the previous pages and a conclusion drawn from them. Since it is intended as a condensed exposition of the metaphysical basis of Euripidean ethics, I give it, for the sake of clarity, in schematic form:

THESIS. Right action is κατὰ φύσιν. Every action παρὰ φύσιν is detrimental to the agent, and therefore wrong.

DEFINITION. φύσις, or the order of nature, includes:
(a) The material and physical laws of the universe.
(b) The material growth, maintenance, and decay of organisms, i.e., life in all its forms.
(c) The cause of those sudden unintelligible (because unprognosticable) events which the ordinary man calls chance or fate.

---

[85] Fr. 444; 509.　　　　　　　　　[87] Fr. 305.
[86] Hipp. 428–30.　　　　　　　　　[88] Fr. 61.

EVIDENCE. Under each of these three aspects of φύσις, our thesis must be shown to be true and operative:

(a) Experience amply shows that man must conform himself to the universal material laws and not seek to divert them from their normal function.

(b) The thesis is manifestly valid for plants and for animals. In the case of man, however, it needs proof:

Every violation of a norm can be measured quantitatively, i.e., it is due either to excess or to deficiency. The norm itself (which our thesis identifies with right conduct) is therefore a mean between two extremes.

We must show that:

(1) Observance of the mean is good for the agent.

The proof is derived from the evident formal and material superiority of all organisms under their complete natural conditions.

(2) Violation of the mean is bad for the agent.

For it throws the organism into an abnormal state in which it is less fitted to perform its function. In man, this is obviously true for his more violent emotional states. There are, however, cases where excess seems to benefit the individual at the expense of his surroundings, particularly at the expense of his fellow-men. Such conduct is manifestly harmful to the latter; but it must be shown to be ultimately harmful to the agent also. No evidence of this is immediately forthcoming, and the proof must be postponed for the moment.

(c) Empirical observation of the unprognosticable events of "chance" and "fate" reveals certain clearly regulated tendencies and proves these very events to be a great and invisible legislation for maintaining the validity of our thesis, and furnishes the proof which we were unable to give at the end of the previous section. We call these events the working of divine justice: the force behind them we identify with the gods.

Thus, our thesis has been shown valid in each of the three aspects of φύσις, and may fairly be considered established.   '

CHAPTER III

THE connection between ethics and theology was not as manifest in Greek as it is in Christian ethics; yet to thinking minds the moral and the religious could not long remain unrelated. Socratic teaching put moral life into Ionian materialistic speculation. The "atheist" helped to rehabilitate the gods. For Euripides the gods are the unseen legislators of the world, who so order the apparent caprices of events that they form a moral system of punishment and reward. Yet Euripides apparently casts discredit on the Olympians. Thus, the Ion shows Apollo taking precariously elaborate measures in order to emerge with even superficial credit from a rather disgraceful scrape. In another play, Herakles complains bitterly against Hera's persecution: Zeus was unfaithful, Hera was jealous, and unoffending Herakles must suffer. "Who would pray to such a goddess?" he exclaims.[1] In the Bacchae, Dionysos takes a hideous revenge, such as mortals scarce approve.[2]

Of all the gods, Apollo suffers most from Euripides. He is vindictive and unforgiving in the Andromache,[3] immoral and underhanded in the Ion,[4] an instigator of mischief in the Suppliants.[5] It may be that there was an Athenian quarrel against the Delphic oracle. It may be that Euripides disbelieved in oracles and divination. His characters exclaim not infrequently against such practices.[6] In the Elektra and the Orestes, the Delphic oracle prompted the murder of Klytaimestra, and Orestes blames all his consequent misfortunes on the god,[7] and Elektra joins in his censure.[8] But here in the end Apollo proves himself just, as Orestes gladly acknowledges.[9] The divine will was slow in accomplishment, — a signal characteristic, as Orestes himself declared.[10] In fact, it is τοιοῦτον φύσει.

I cannot enter in detail into the question of Euripides' religion;

[1] H. M. 1307–10; cf. 1316–20 and 339–47.
[2] Bacch. 1348.   [3] Andr. 1161–5.
[4] Ion, passim; cf. esp. Ion's own criticisms of Apollo in 436–51; 355; 367.
[5] Hik. 138 and 219–22.
[6] E.g. Hel. 744–8; 756–60. But cf. Hipp. 1320–4.
[7] Or. 285–7; 414–20; 591–9; El. 971–3; 981; cf. 1245–6.
[8] Or. 162–4.   [9] Or. 1666–7.   [10] Or. 420.

but must be content with the assertion that all the evidence seems to me to indicate quite clearly that Euripides is so severe with the gods because he believes in them so thoroughly. From the often quoted fragment:

εἰ θεοί τι δρῶσιν αἰσχρόν, οὐκ εἰσὶν θεοί,
"If the gods do evil, then they are not gods,"

(From Fragment 294)

we must not conclude that there are no gods, but that the gods do no evil. The quarrel with Apollo is the only serious instance to the contrary, and this seems to be directed against the Delphic oracle for other than ethical reasons.

For, if there is to be any higher ethical sanction for mankind, the forces of the universal ordinance cannot be evil or do evil. For this reason, the gods must be purged of all their traditional immoralities. The gods can do no evil, and therefore Euripides is merciless with them. But he fights for them not against them:

οὐδένα γὰρ οἶμαι δαιμόνων εἶναι κακόν.

(I. T. 391)

Euripides openly declares that the gods must be purged of their evil reputations and established as that higher justice from which human morality derives its sanction. Therefore, the gods should be above revenge[11] and more wisely forgiving than mankind.[12] In a word, they can do no evil;[13] for otherwise we, who imitate them, would not be to blame for the evil which we perform,[14] since our actions take their sanction from the gods.[15] Thus the gods must be moral and just, for otherwise where should we turn for justice?[16] If there are gods at all, the just man will gain a good reward[17] and the wicked be destroyed,[18] but if there are no gods, all justice vanishes, and why should we strive to be moral?[19] Or, reversing the argument, if injustice prevails on earth, we cannot believe in the gods;[20] but "when I see the wicked fallen, I say, The race of gods exists!" (Fr. 581). In one form or another, so say most of the heroes and heroines of Euripides' plays; and, presumably, so said also the Athenian audience which beheld the

---

[11] Bacch. 1348.   [12] Hipp. 120.
[13] Fr. 294 quoted above. Yet Aphrodite often works evil; hence she is not a god, but something else, something more powerful (Hipp. 358-61), who overcomes even the gods (Fr. 434). See below p. 41.   [14] Ion 449-51.
[15] Hipp. 98.   [17] I. A. 1034-5.   [19] I. A. 1035.
[16] Ion 253.   [18] Hik. 505.   [20] El. 583.

ultimate triumph of the good and punishment of the overbearing, of
the wicked who exceeded the due measure of the norm of life.

In conclusion, I give the important passage from the Troiades, which
openly points a finger to the place of the gods in Euripides' ethical
system: [21]

> ὅστις ποτ' εἶ σύ, δυστόπαστος εἰδέναι,
> Ζεύς, εἴτ' ἀνάγκη φύσεος εἴτε νοῦς βροτῶν,
> προσηυξάμην σε· πάντα γὰρ δι' ἀψόφου
> βαίνων κελεύθου κατὰ δίκην τὰ θνήτ' ἄγεις.

(Tro. 885-8)

For Euripides the gods are ceasing to be persons. They are becoming
the more or less abstract forces in Nature which work for universal
justice.

. . . .

Of human justice I can find in Euripides no clear account. He frequently gives it a partial definition. It involves religious observance
and veneration; [22] it is punctiliousness (ἀτρέκεια); [23] it is respect for property; [24] it is altruistic, since it is directed toward the good of fellow-
men. [25] But though naturally we find no analysis and systematic
treatment such as Aristotle gives in the fifth book of the Nicomachean Ethics, there are a couple of passages in Euripides which are
definite.

The first is Iokaste's speech to her two warring sons in the Phoinis-
sai. [26] She is pleading for a divided kingship in Thebes; but appeals
to more general principles: "The tyrant's rule is merely successful
injustice and doomed to anxiety and misfortune. Be not over-ambi-
tious; but rather, be just, and grant everyone his share. Justice is
equality."

The second passage [27] is in similar vein. Theseus is disputing
political theory with the Theban herald for the glorification of Athens

---

[21] A convenient indication of the philosophic echoes in this passage may be found
in J. Adam's *Religious Teachers of Greece*, p. 299 ff., where it may be of interest to
note that the important phrase ἀνάγκη φύσεος draws a blank, so to speak: — "It is
not so clear that Euripides had any definite philosophic theory in view when he suggested that this Zeus or Aether is perhaps to be regarded as ἀνάγκη φύσεος — Nature's
Necessity or Law. He may be thinking, perhaps, of the Atomists, etc. . . ."
Mr. Adam justly suggests that the εἴτε clauses "are not really intended to exclude
one another."

[22] Herakl. 901-3; cf. Fr. 1063. [25] Herakl. 1-5.
[23] Fr. 92. [26] Phoin. 528-67.
[24] Fr. 356. [27] Hik. 429-55; v. also Fr. 429.

and the delectation of the audience. He condemns tyranny and commends written law, whereby rich and poor, and strong and weak, have equal hearing and equal redress. Such equality is justice.

But though there is neither adequate definition nor analytic discussion of justice in Euripides such as Plato gives in his Republic or Aristotle in the fifth book of the Ethics, indirectly there is evidence of ideals as thoughtful and as far-reaching.

As we have seen, he believes that justice is the gods' care and obtains a deep and universal self-fulfilment. Though occasional characters cry out that rapacious and ruthless power is so successful and complain:

πόλεις τε μικρὰς οἶδα τιμώσας θεούς,
αἳ μειζόνων κλύουσι δυσσεβεστέρων
λόγχης ἀριθμῷ πλείονος κρατούμεναι,

(From Fragment 288)

yet the conviction is strong that

οὐδεὶς στρατεύσας ἄδικα σῶς ἦλθεν πάλιν,

(Fragment 355)

and " foolish are they who gather virtue with the point of the spear; if battle is to decide, never will strife depart from cities of mankind."[28] In fact, it is entirely due to evil of man that there is injustice abroad; for "the gods' deeds are just, but among wicked men they sicken and fall into confusion." [29]

The hidden world works for justice, for equality among men, and for requital of good and evil. Kingship and tyranny must vanish and a perfect equality arise among men. With such an ideal, what of women and of slaves?

Euripides had a profound belief in women.[30] He did not look on them as Plato in the interest of formal theorising once seems to have done,[31] as men with child-bearing functions, able to do all that men could, though hampered by a lack of strength. Euripides looked on

---

[28] Chorus in Hel. 1151-7.

[29] Fr. 609. The reading is more uncertain than the general trend.

[30] The long speech against women by Hippolytos (615–68) accords with an anti-erotic or sexually perverted nature. It throws no light on Euripides' own views. Rather, it shows much understanding of a type which has probably always been exceptional, but which has always existed. Of the other misogynistic outbursts in Euripides, I find five are mere short fragments without a background (Fr. 500; 532; 805; 1045; 1046). There remains the taunt of Jason in Med. 573–5, which is scarcely a rooted conviction of either author or character. For a good survey of the material, v. Decharme, ch. IV, § 1.   [31] Rep. Book V.

women quite frankly as women. He saw many faults in them, that they were scheming and unscrupulous,[32] inordinately jealous,[33] defective in a sense of honour and fair play,[34] gossiping and meddlesome.[35] Yet he declares a good wife to be the bulwark of a house [36] and a blessing to the fortunate man who wedded her.[37] But women are not men disguised under another sex. Their virtues are womanly, their natural functions are essentially domestic.[38] But justice and equality apply as much to them as to men. They have been unfairly criticised, good women and bad have fallen under a common censure;[39] it is men who have talked, while women have had no hearing;[40] had they but equal opportunity, they could recount as many evils about men.[41] They should have equality of speech, therefore. More than that, divorce should be a mutual right [42] and unchastity as much an offence in the husband as in the wife.[43]

It is part, therefore, of Euripides' belief in that equality which he identifies with justice, that women should have equal rights with men, provided always that they fulfil their place as women.[44] It is of course consonant with this that polygamy, being unequal, is unjust and unnatural. In the Andromache, the chorus compares a household with two wives to a city with two rulers, a play by two authors, and a ship with two pilots.[45]

In the case of slaves, Euripides feels none of the injustice of their position. It is not that they are morally worthless. Though he sometimes calls them so,[46] more often he shows a great appreciation of their self-respect, their honour, and their faithfulness. The old nurses in the Medeia and the Hippolytos are among his most human and attract-

[32] Med. 407–9; I. T. 1032; Hik. 294; Andr. 262–8; 380–4; 425–32, where Hermione seems to be the instigator; but much of the Andromache must be discounted as a ruthless attack on Spartan behaviour.
[33] Andr. 155–80. [35] Phoin. 198–201.
[34] Fr. 673; Andr. 516–22. [36] Fr. 1041.
[37] Fr. 164; 1042; 1043; cf. I. A. 749–50.
[38] Praise of good wives: Fr. 819; 820; Tro. 645–56; and esp. Fr. 901.
[39] Ion 398–400; Hek. 1183–6; Fr. 496; 658; cf. Fr. 497.
[40] Ion 1090–8.
[41] Med. 421–30. Cf. on the unequal and difficult position of men, Medeia's speech in 230–51. [42] Andr. 672–4.
[43] El. 1036–41. Cf. however the opposite attitude of Andromache in the play of that name, 215–26.
[44] They should remain indoors, Herakl. 476–7; Fr. 525; and not strive to rule in their home, Andr. 213–4; El. 1052–3.
[45] Andr. 464–85. Cf. the equally strong opinion of Hermione in the same play, 173–80.
[46] Cf. Fr. 49; 50; 215; and the Phrygian in the latter part of the Orestes.

ive characters. In fact, in three instances he declares them at least
the equals of their masters.[47] Yet he never cries out against the injustice of their position. I imagine that he, like Aristotle, must have looked
on slavery as a natural and necessary institution. He never expresses
the possibility of doing without it. Its evils and injustice never touch
his logic or brain; but that they could touch his heart, and call forth his
deepest emotions of pity and sorrow, is patent to any who read even
casually the great lamentations in the Hekabe and Troiades.

Slavery is a misfortune, the greatest of all misfortunes, so hopeless
that death is preferable to it.[48] Yet there is nothing to be done. It is
the order of nature and the will of the unseen ordinance. This seems
to be Euripides' position; but under its reasoning we seem to hear
his soul crying out with the distress of Hekabe, yet comforting itself
with the thought that under good masters the lot of the slaves was not
evil, and that in the household of Alkestis they were rather children
than serfs.[49] It is rather the horrors of war, such as we see them in the
Hekabe, that lend their gloomy colours to the spectacle of man become
the chattel and the property of his fellow-beings. It is a strange position, humanity struggling for expression almost against the dictate
of reason.

At the beginning of this thesis I spoke of an ἀρχή, a universal principle, running through Greek ethical thought. This ἀρχή I identified
with life in the norm of Nature. To Euripides, a careful interrogation
of Nature supplies the empiric rules of conduct, and so furnishes an
objective standard, external to the agent. What behaviour is right in
this or that crisis? what are the gods? what is the proper position of
women or of slaves? To answer these and other questions of conduct,
we must in every case turn to Nature. What is the φύσις of women and
of slaves? we must ask.[50] If that can be determined, we shall have

---

[47] Hel. 728–31; Ion 854–6; Fr. 515.
[48] Hek. 357–78; 211–15. Fr. 247.   [49] Alk. 193–5, 769–71.
[50] It will be noticed that this question implies a classification by type, as if woman
qua woman had a distinctive φύσις. This process of thinking by type or class is
natural to a people among whom the caste-system prevails. But it is also in general
a necessary stage in a process of differentiation. One is reminded of the development of artistic types in sculpture, from the undifferentiated nude male to the various
distinct athletic types (the boxer, the wrestler, the runner, etc.), at which still unin-
dividualised stage the process seems almost arrested until the fourth century. In
much the same way, the Greek thinkers differentiated the moral agent into types or
classes, whose functions and natural capacities (ἔργον and φύσις) they treated as
limited and distinctive. So the slave, δοῦλος (Soph. O. C. 763–4), the νομεύς (*ib.*
1118; cf. Od. 17, 322).

discovered their proper position and conduct. The appeal to φύσις is the great source of moral sanction. Whatever is κατὰ φύσιν is morally right; whatever is παρὰ φύσιν is morally wrong.

To the Greek mind, therefore, morality is not a matter of subjective impulse or conscience or self-interrogation. Man identifies himself in the world by a realization that he is an ordered part of it with a determined place and function. It is his duty to fulfil that function, to play his part as Nature intended.

This is the ἀνυπόθετος ἀρχή of which I spoke. It has proved itself under all of Euripides' ethical feeling as the *forma informans* which alone explains and unifies his teaching. His religion, his morality, the meaning of his plays, all become clearer in the light of this single and simple principle. Thus understood, the Greek tragedian is as logical and as consistent as his fellow Greeks in philosophy and art.

The thesis is therefore concluded, — or rather, it would be, were it not that there is another and counter principle in Euripides which conflicts with this one and in certain cases supersedes it. To this other principle the remainder of the thesis must be devoted.

CHAPTER IV

UNDER a system of ethics such as we have sketched, the individual is self-centred. His actions are not for others, but for himself. In identifying his own complete and harmonious development with his highest good, he excludes that long range of so-called Christian virtues which stretches from self-denial to self-obliteration. For how can it help the individual, if he die to save another than himself?

Yet human instincts and human nature have always been much the same, and the Greek could die for his city or lay down his life for a friend, whether or not strict logic of his ethical theories justified his behaviour. Nor could he withhold his admiration and applause if he beheld another man perform similar unselfish acts.

In the Nicomachean Ethics we read nothing about self-sacrifice. For such an unwearied student as Aristotle, devoted to increasing his knowledge and extending his logic till it should cover every phase of human thought and action, what possible attraction or what possible meaning could there be in a creed of self-abnegation whose commands must run counter to his whole life's activity? With the instincts of the scholar, however, Aristotle combined those of a teacher, and here he experienced the desire of labouring for another's benefit. There creeps into the Aristotelian ethics, therefore, the famous chapter on friendship, with its characteristic analysis of friends into three kinds, friends for delectation, friends for utility, and friends for love of the good which is in them. The last class contains the only true friends. This meant, in the fourth century before Christ, to Aristotle, tutor of Alexander and sage of the Lyceum, three kinds of associates, — men to dine with and to jest with; influential men with power in their hands; and, last, the true intimates, pupils and followers, who could discuss philosophy. Now, philosophy among the Greeks was not a lone man's plaything, a solitary invention of secluded minds. Truth rose only out of discussion; like a child, it needed two parents. The outcome of the Nicomachean Ethics is a glorification of the life of philosophic speculation and an admission of the need of like-minded friends for successful pursuit of this philosophic ideal. To the last, therefore, Aristotle clung to the self-centred creed of the scholar, admitting friends not for friends'

38

sake, but because they were indispensable to that highest scholarly and philosophical self-development which was for him the consummate human type on earth, the realization of all the latent possibilities of the thinking animal, man.[1]

It is interesting to see how every distinction in Aristotle's discussion of friendship can be found already made in Euripides. Thus, there are the same classes of false friends, those for advantage,[2] and those through pleasure (ἡδονῇ,[3] πρὸς χάριν [4]), and such friendships may exist among evil men through the attraction of like for like,[5] while true friendship occurs only between the good, for it is a "love for a just and restrained and virtuous soul" (ἔρως ψυχῆς δικαίας σώφρονός τε κἀγαθῆς).[6] Misfortune is the great test of friendship, for it reveals the motive, and only that friendship which is based, not on advantage or an idle interest, but on a deep-rooted affection will endure amid adversity.[7] Such friends are a gift beyond all value.[8] Though they are admittedly rare,[9] there are eloquent and unforgettable examples in the pages of Euripides. Such is the friendship of Theseus and Herakles in the Herakles Mainomenos. Insanity and murder with all its pollution do not shake the loyalty of Theseus, who proclaims for friendship a higher sanctity:

$$\text{οὐδεὶς ἀλάστωρ τοῖς φίλοις ἐκ τῶν φίλων.}$$

(H. M. 1234) [10]

The last lines of the play [11] mark still more the sanctity and solemnity of this high friendship which no crime can shatter or alter. More famous, though not more touching, is the indissoluble comradeship of Orestes and Pylades throughout the Tauric Iphigeneia, the Elektra, and the Orestes. Of such a friendship must have been written the Fragment from which a line has already been quoted. Though it is not

---

[1] The ἕτερος αὐτός is a logical quibble to keep the ethical centre within the individual. An unselfish act for a friend now ceases to be unselfish, for the action is performed to benefit that more comprehensive Self (I plus friend, or Self plus Second Self). The strict logic of individualistic ethics is preserved, but the barriers are really already down. Why limit the extension of self to a friend or two? But if the extension is unlimited, there is no longer any individualistic ethic.

[2] H. M. 1224–5; Fr. 465; Hek. 1227.

[3] Fr. 298, l. 2.   [5] Ib. 298; 809.

[4] Ib. 364, ll. 19–20.   [6] Ib. 342.

[7] Euripides calls such friends φίλοι σαφεῖς (Or. 1155; H. M. 55; Fr. 928), ἀληθεῖς (Hik. 867; Hipp. 927), ὀρθῶς (Andr. 377; H. M. 56).

[8] Or. 727–8; 804–6; 1155–7; H. M. 1425–6; Fr. 7; 928.

[9] El. 605–7; Hik. 867–8; Fr. 736.

[10] In Or. 793–4 Pylades holds the same belief toward the frenzy of Orestes.

[11] H. M. 1394 ff.

particularly good poetry, it has enough ethical import to justify its quotation in full:

φίλος γὰρ ἦν μοι, καὶ μ᾽ ἔρως ἕλοι ποτὲ [12]
οὐκ εἰς τὸ μῶρον, οὐδέ μ᾽ εἰς Κύπριν τρέπων.
ἀλλ᾽ ἔστι δή τις ἄλλος ἐν βροτοῖς ἔρως
ψυχῆς δικαίας σώφρονός τε κἀγαθῆς.
καὶ χρῆν δὲ τοῖς βροτοῖσιν τόνδ᾽ εἶναι νόμον,
τῶν εὐσεβούντων οἵτινές γε σώφρονες
ἐρᾶν, Κύπριν δὲ τὴν Διὸς χαίρειν ἐᾶν.

(Fragment 342)

The Aristotelian friend is part of the self-centred ethical system; but in this Euripidean fragment, and in the lover-like comradeship of Orestes and Pylades, of Theseus and Herakles, a new element has crept in, too strong for "system," an element which threatens the clarity of the Euripidean logic with the colouring of a fatal emotion.

It will be noted that in such a form of individualism there is no room for the rather self-destructive enlargement which classes altruism as a higher form of selfishness. Euripides could not logically claim that self-sacrifice was also κατὰ φύσιν and therefore commendable, any more than, for example, a gardener could claim that the extermination of the tare to give soil to the corn was *for the tare* κατὰ φύσιν. As long as immortality and a higher, external moral sanction are not involved, the individual is to be considered entirely as a material manifestation, here and now, closely analogous to any other living product of nature, whose end, and therefore, in a thinking being, whose "duty," is realization of form (in the sense of complete attainment of εἶδος). Self-sacrifice is in consequence eminently παρὰ φύσιν.

We must constantly remember this distinction between ancient naturalistic individualism and certain modern rehabilitations which can conveniently merge the individual into a "higher self" by a pleasantly indefinite transition. If we insist on our rather humble analogies and argue as if man were merely an intelligent political animal, akin to other natural forms, these rather insidious sophistications lose their force, while we ourselves shall be closer to the attitude of mind of Sokrates, with his constant adjudication of ethical problems by concrete analogies in the lowly trades and crafts, and of Aristotle, whose pregnant use of such concepts as ἔργον, τέλος, δύναμις, and εἶδος, I have throughout tried to copy.

[12] The reading is corrupt.

In friendships of this extreme and beautiful sort, then, the ethical postulate is in danger. Curiously enough in that other, and to our thought more intense, emotional relation, the love of man and woman, this is seldom true. Making all allowance for ethopoiia, for the difficulty of distinguishing the *dramatis personae* from Euripides' own utterance, such is the consistency of sentiment that it seems hard to resist the conclusion that Euripides looked on sexual love as a violent and irrational thing,[13] an intruder into an otherwise ordered world. It is mere folly:

$$τὰ \ μῶρα \ γὰρ \ πάντ' \ ἐστὶν \ 'Αφροδίτη \ βροτοῖς,$$
$$καὶ \ τοὔνομ' \ ὀρθῶς \ ἀφροσύνης \ ἄρχει \ θεᾶς.$$

(Tro. 989–90)

Running counter to that great system of morality and justice which Euripides calls "the gods," Aphrodite cannot be herself a god. She is something even more powerful.[14] She is quietly excluded from the ethical system as an irrational and uncontrollable factor.

But this other love, that bound Pylades and Orestes, caught the Greek imagination where the more ordinary love of man and woman failed. Too sane and wise to be irrational, too abiding to be fortuitous or merely fleeting and uncontrollable, it demanded with full right a place in the Greek ethical system, and such a place the self-centred creed, with which we have been dealing, was unable to give.

Love in still another form impressed Euripides with its strength and its beauty. "To all men, children are their very soul," says Andromache.[15] It is not a question of the pleasure which they give us. Although to some they are more to be desired than wealth or kingly power,[16] others may judge themselves happier without children, for they may sicken and die or grow into evil ways and, all in all, cause only care and grief.[17] But virtuous and wicked men alike love their children;[18] and there is nothing more intimate than the bond between parents and their children,[19] nor any sweeter love than that of mother and child.[20] And out of the strength of such love comes self-sacrifice, the obliteration of the individual for the sake of another.

In the Herakleidai, Makaria dies of her own will, in order to save her brothers. She justifies her act by a long speech, claiming that, first, justice demands her sacrifice; Marathon has received her and her

---

[13] Fr. 139.
[14] Hipp. 359–60.
[15] Andr. 418.
[16] Ion 485–91.
[17] Chorus in Med. 1090–1115; Admetos in Alk. 879–88; Fr. 575.
[18] H. M. 634–6.
[19] Fr. 333.
[20] Fr. 360.

brothers as suppliants at the risk of its prosperity and its freedom, hence she must take equal dangers on herself to save Marathon;[21] secondly, not to die would show lack of courage and bring shame upon her;[22] thirdly, the alternative, life, is not preferable, since she would not attain happiness;[23] and therefore, in final conclusion, it is better for her to die with honour, since to live is shameful.[24] In all this inhuman reasoning, how the ethical logician is trying to find a place for self-sacrifice in his "system!" Makaria may make this forensic speech; yet she acts through impulse and for love of her brothers, not through logic or for reason. Euripides admits as much. He makes Makaria realise that the deed, to be good, must come from love and not through any restraint. When Iolaos suggests that she should draw lots with her sisters to determine the victim, she refuses, and even intimates that should she be commanded by the fall of the lot, she would resist such a death; for it would resemble an execution more than a deed of virtue.[25] And thereby she shows that her harangue was a judicial gloss, hiding her true motive of voluntary self-devotion to save those whom she loves. In that admission, the individualistic creed of ethics breaks down. It is not shame and honour that are the motives. The individual is no longer consulting the interests of his own harmonious and complete self-development. But to do so was the fundamental demand of the system which we have been developing.

There are numerous other cases in Euripides, for the situation makes a great appeal to the dramatic instinct and that human sympathy which a great tragic poet possesses. Andromache is unhesitatingly prepared to die in order to save her son Molossos.[26] Hekabe wishes to take the place of her daughter whom the Greeks have voted for sacrifice to the shade of Achilles.[27] Alkestis, dying that her husband may live, is a familiar figure in all men's minds.[28] So, too, Iphigeneia's sacrifice is voluntary. When the plot becomes involved, so that apparently bloodshed and intestine strife must break out in the Greek camp at Aulis, Iphigeneia suddenly claims her right to die in behalf of the Greek cause against Troy. She has been weeping and lamenting in childish fashion: all at once, she understands her duty and her privilege, — "To all Greece didst thou bear me!"[29]

---

[21] Her. 503–10.   [24] Ib. 525–8.   [27] Hek. 385–7.
[22] Ib. 515–19.   [25] Ib. 547–51.
[23] Ib. 520–4.   [26] Andr. 406–18.
[28] Cf. also the more difficult situation in the long fragment from the Erechtheus quoted by Lycurgus (Kata Leokr. 100), where the mother gives her son to die to save her country.   [29] I. A. 1386.

So far does the power of affection reach, that even where nothing is gained, the sacrifice is offered. In the Helena, husband and wife, precariously reunited, vow to die together if both may not live:

Ελ. ψαύω, θανόντος σοῦ τόδ' ἐκλείψειν φάος.

Με. κἀγὼ στερηθεὶς σοῦ τελευτήσειν βίον.

(Hel. 839–40)

In the Orestes, Pylades insists on dying if his friend Orestes must, however needless the sacrifice seems.[30] His, also, are the stirring lines:

μήθ' αἷμά μου δέξαιτο κάρπιμον πέδον,
μὴ λαμπρὸς αἰθήρ, εἴ σ' ἐγὼ προδούς ποτε
ἐλευθερώσας τοὐμὸν ἀπολίποιμι σέ.

(Or. 1086–8)

I have tried to show that the Greek individualistic ethic is incompatible with certain emotions which we class among the higher Christian virtues, and that precisely these emotions occur in Euripides. When, as in the cases just cited, life is freely and gladly given for another's sake, not out of selfish interest or a weighing of For and Against, but out of love, whether of country or of wife or of friend, the fundamental ethical thesis has been violated. The individual proceeds to efface his entire existence, and, with it, all possibility of further realising his spiritual and bodily powers. It seems to me a significant comment on all individualistic ethics that even in so logical and successful an exemplification as that of fourth-century Greek morality, though the philosopher could be self-consistent, the more human tragedian — for all his sense for logic — was driven into violating the cardinal principle of his ethical system.

This observation has its bearing on modern conditions of thought and feeling, as I intend to show. But before sketching the change of attitude in ethics since Aristotle, I wish to add at least a brief note of comparison between that philosopher and Euripides. It is almost a commonplace of Aristotelian criticism to scent an odour of the comic stage in the ethical characters so drastically and dramatically portrayed in the central books of the Nicomachean Ethics. I offer the general tenor of this essay as an indication that Aristotle's total indebtedness to the stage is still more thoroughgoing. A system such as Euripides held needs only to be subjected to the rigorous formalising of the Aristotelian logic — and the Nicomachean Ethics, as Burnet has shown,[31]

---

[30] Or. 1069–72.   [31] In his edition of the Ethics.

is full of logical formalism — and to be interpreted in the light of
the Aristotelian psychology of conduct, to produce almost the entire
fabric of the Nicomachean Ethics.[32] There is the same fundamental
assumption — a monstrous *non sequitur* of optimism — that, because the
fulfilment of function is the aim of every organism considered as part
of Nature, therefore it is also the aim or end of man as a self-con-
scious self-directed individual, and thus the best thing for him to do;
and being best, it is thus equivalent to the Highest Good. The εὐδαιμονία
of Book I is Aeschylean-Herodotean preaching on the transiency of
prosperity, the unreliability of τὰ ἔξω ἀγαθά reconciled as far as possible
with the equation of right action to action in the norm of Nature.[33]
The immediately following books contain the explanation of the mechanism of such action — the psychological mediation between the intellectual act of apprehending the general ethical law and the practical act
of conduct in the concrete. This psychological mediation effected by
the doctrine of προαίρεσις, and the divisions of the sentient activities,
could not, I admit, have been found ready-made in the Attic drama.
But it is not part of the moral theory, so much as of the scientific analysis of the mechanism of behaviour. The more properly speculative distinction between ἕξις and ἐνέργεια, however, is already in Euripides;
at least, the equivalent doctrine that there is no well-being without
well-doing seems clear in the following fragment from the Antiope:

εἰ δ' εὐτυχῶν τις καὶ βίον κεκτημένος
μηδὲν δόμοισι τῶν καλῶν πειράσεται,
ἐγὼ μὲν οὔποτ' αὐτὸν ὄλβιον καλῶ,
φύλακα δὲ μᾶλλον χρημάτων εὐδαίμονα.

Is not this precisely the point of Aristotle's definition of Eudaimonia
in Book I? Following this psychological treatise, come the practical

[31] On the other hand, the examination in this thesis has afforded hardly any
Platonic doctrine. Is not this merely another indication that Plato was a highly
original (or, at any rate, a highly specialised) thinker, whereas Aristotle was a school-
logician and analytic encyclopaedist working from the normal viewpoint of the
ordinary educated Athenian?

[33] Cf. with Aristotle's account, the following Euripidean treatment of Eudaimonia: It is transient and uncertain (Herakl. 609–18, Hipp. 981–2), and we can call
no man happy before death (Andr. 100–2, Herakl. 865–6). No man is completely
happy (Med. 1224–30; Fr. 46; 196). None are happy without aid of the gods
(Fr. 149; Her. 609), and none are happy unless they are prosperous. For this prosperity (τὰ ἔξω ἀγαθά), children are necessary (Andr. 418–20) and wealth is necessary
(Erech. 16–17). Without opportunity it is impossible to perfect and develop one-
self (Fr. 738). Finally, happiness is essentially an activity, for there is no well-being
without well-doing (Fr. 198).

rules for right conduct, centred and contained in the doctrine of the
Mean, — the very rule-of-life which has been brought out so vividly
by our study of Euripides. Then follow the "pre-Theophrastean"
characters, vivid attempts at *ethopoiia*, and redolent of practical play-
writing. The exhaustive treatment of justice in Book V echoes mathe-
matical theorists and is not exemplified in Euripides; but just because
it is so largely a mere practical calculus for the juryman, its purely
ethical content is slight. The discussion of wisdom, pleasure, and
incontinence is a more purely speculative heritage from the Sophists
and the Academy. The nature of friendship is already in Euripides in
strikingly Aristotelian form.

I conclude, therefore, that we estimate Aristotle's Ethics wrongly
if we treat it as moral speculation. The morality came to his hand
from the Sophists and the stage. Out of it, he made a practical exposition of human behaviour. The Nicomachean Ethics is not a treatise
on Duty or Obligation or Moral Sanction, but a text-book of psychology
with practical hints on conduct.

POSTSCRIPT ON INDIVIDUALISTIC SYSTEMS

THE Greek civilisation perfected itself within rather narrow geographical bounds. In the fourth century before Christ it began to affect non-Greek people. Alexander the Great gave a whirlwind impulse to a movement already begun. By the third century it was widely disseminated through the Mediterranean lands. In extending its application it naturally was modified to meet non-Greek conditions. Its art and literature and material code of life met with severe change, but endured the test triumphantly; but its ethic failed. At least, it failed in that form which the Athenian drama had taught and Aristotle had systematised. City-life grew enormously in these Hellenistic days. The great towns, like magnets, drew people from the farm and its empty routine to the energetic idleness of the splendid city-streets. The extremes of society worked ever further apart. The idle rich and the mob-swelling poor now first appear as outstanding social factors. With the increased disparity of level, luxury and want, enjoyment and misery are more emphatic and more prominent. The poor and wretched cry out that life is a succession of insupportable evils. The rich revel in goldsmith's ware and marble-coated houses, in feasting and fine apparel. What meaning for either of them has the old fifth-century advice to develop the Self harmoniously and evenly in order to realize all the inherent potentialities of the organic life which Nature gave us? Especially to the ill-clothed and ill-fed rabble, this would seem a high-flown and senseless creed. Something else was needed; Stoicism and Epicureanism swept the Hellenistic world. The one thought life full of evil and counselled a high fortitude as man's best armour. The other saw that enjoyment was still possible and counselled gathering the roses while we may. Whatever the original philosophy of these creeds, this seems to have been their practical application. In this form they fitted their world and gained their votaries. But both talk much of φύσις, especially Stoicism (though neither can gladly and completely acquiesce in it); and both must be studied genetically as divergent growths out of the ethical system which Euripides exemplifies.

This earlier ethic hinged on self-assertion. It was applicable to a prosperous community, an aristocracy whose material needs were guaranteed by slavery. The doctrine had no application to this slave-class

46

itself and was in fact never extended to them even in the broadest theorising. When an ethic was needed which would apply to both classes — and for that matter to all mankind — the Greek system failed. The necessity of that failure is foreshadowed in Euripides. Constant preoccupation with tragic situations developed in him a sympathy for the unfortunate and an understanding of their suffering which is completely lacking in the theorising self-absorption of Aristotle. From the poet we learn what we should never have guessed from the philosopher, that the Greek ethic, though logically consistent for ordinary Greek conditions, in extreme human crises breaks down. An ethical study of Euripides is consequently of considerable interest because it defines the range of conditions within which an individualistic ethic can be self-consistent and satisfactory. Now, many of these conditions, after being lost in Hellenistic, Roman, and Christian times, have reappeared in the very recent world of to-day. For the first time in centuries, we can apply the lesson of Greek ethics to ourselves.

As I understand the matter, a fundamental difference between Greek and Christian ethics derives from the source of moral sanction. Christian dogma, I presume, reflects the legal tone of Roman civil administration and Hebraic religious law: it is essentially imposed, like a *corpus juridicum*, by an authority external to the individual. Christ and Caesar are parallel manifestations, to each of whom must be rendered what is his due and whatever is demanded by the laws whose administration ultimately pinnacles in them. In Christian law the emphasis shifts from this world to the world hereafter. There is thus a marked difference from Greek ethical thought.

In general, I should formulate the matter thus: Where there is the belief in a personal creative Deity and in individual immortality, there must arise an external non-earthly sanction; without these beliefs, the interest must centre in the individual, in the living intelligent Being, here and now. In the latter case, in a complex community, Hedonism or Stoicism arises as a personal guide to life, with Utilitarianism, perhaps, as a more impersonal theoretical system; while in a closed aristocracy or a socialistic community, the Euripidean and Aristotelian Individualism will make their appeal.

Now that modern wide-spread prosperity has removed much of the need for self-suppression, a material condition reappears wherein each may to some extent live for himself and develop his own faculties to the utmost. Harmonious and complete development of the various physical

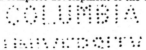

and intellectual faculties once more becomes the aim in education. Hence also there is an ever more marked wane of sympathy with some of the fundamental teachings of Christian dogma, just because self-development implies self-assertion and an individualistic rather than altruistic attitude. In political as well as pedagogical theory the same trend is apparent. Socialism, in its general tenets, makes unbroken progress. It aims at an increased efficiency in the community, and, for its ideal, would give every individual the opportunity to realise his highest possibilities in the social fabric. What is this but the great doctrine of Greek ethics applied to a more complex community? Under a completely triumphant socialism — if the realisation be practicable — our attitude would approximate that of the Greeks; provided that we had sufficient sense for form and balance to keep us from the degeneration of excesses. To keep this sense alert and operative was, as we have seen, the main occupation and value of Greek ethical teaching.

Obviously, self-development can be easily confused with self-interestedness. A self-centred attitude may degenerate into greed and callow selfishness. Its true character as a high moral system can only be maintained by a people who realise intuitively that perfection does not mean the quantitatively greatest, but a difficult and rather subtle balance between the Too Much and the Too Little. Surely Euripides realised that for the Greeks this dangerous mistake was possible. Else why, with all his bold innovations, did he cling so strongly to the old dramatic theme and show, as rigorously as Aeschylus himself, that every man however wealthy or well-born, if he confuse self-development with self-aggrandisement at the expense of others, is punished by the great law of universal justice with which the gods are merged and into which they disappear.

CPSIA information can be obtained
at www.ICGtesting.com
Printed in the USA
LVOW13s1555091017
551761LV00013B/666/P